INK-INC PUBLISHING

A Dance With Romeo

Mary Hymers was born in 1927 at Winlaton, a small village within the parish of Ryton in the northeast of England. At the age of fourteen she began work at Sinclair's Tobacco Factory on Westgate Road in Newcastle where she continued to work until her marriage; a marriage ban against employment was in place for women at that time. After the birth of her son, Mary returned to work and took on a variety of jobs within the village in which she lived, the local nature of her employment enabling her to keep house in the tradition in which she had been raised while still being able to contribute to the family's income. In 2001, at the age of seventy-four, she decided to write her life. A Dance With Romeo is the first book of her memoirs and describes her early childhood and teenage years during the Second World War and ends with her marriage to Teofilius Yakubovksis and the birth of her son.

A Dance With Romeo
by
Mary Hymers

Ink-Inc Publishing Book N⁰ 6
Published by Ink-Inc Publishing Ltd

First Published Nov 2017
©Mary Hymers all rights reserved

Cover Design by Ink-Inc Publishing Ltd
Front cover photograph ©Mary Hymers 2017
Back photograph ©Mary Hymers 2017

Mary Hymers asserts the moral right to be
identified as the author of this work.

www.ink-inc-publishing.com
inkspiration@ink-inc-publishing.com

ISBN 978-0-9934444-5-6

All rights reserved. No part of this publication may be reproduced,
stored in a retrieval system, or transmitted in any form or by
any means, electronic, mechanical, photocopying or otherwise,
without the prior written permission of the publisher.

To my family.

With all my love & a million kisses.

Contents

1. My Family 1
2. Our New House 8
3. Blaydon Burn 15
4. School & Play 20
5. Granny Gilfillan 26
6. My Father's Family 33
7. Winlaton Village 36
8. A Rumour of War 46
9. The Wars Still Going On 53
10. 2 Years & Getting Complicated 61
11. The War's Still On 68
12. No More Jeeps 77
13. A Trip To London 83
14. Sinclairs Tobacco Factory 92
15. The End of the War 96
16. Achim 102
17. A Trip to Sunderland 115
18. A Stranger at the Door 124
19. Goodbye to Achim 133

20.	Oscar	138
21.	The First Dance	146
22.	A Late Night	156
23.	A Trip to Scotland	170
24.	A Borrowed Bicycle	180
25.	The International Dance	184
26.	Tony's Story	193
27.	We Get Married	204

Chapter 1
My Family

My name is Mary Hymers and I was born in the year 1927. My Mother's maiden name was Thomasina Gilfillan; after she married my Father Norman Hymers, she took his surname and became Thomasina Hymers. I have one elder brother Alexander who was the oldest of us, then my sister Barbara, then me, Mary, and the baby of the family was my brother Norman.

But before I tell you my life's story, I am going to take you back to my Mother's side of the family. The Gilfillans had a history dating back to the eighteen hundreds and before. My Granny's name was Emma and her name was Emma Dance before she married my Grandfather. His name was Alexander Gilfillan, although he always got called Sandy for short.

My Mother, Thomasina Gilfillan, had two sisters and two brothers and she would tell you that two others died in their infancy. My Mother's sisters were my Aunt Marie and my Aunt Isabel, and then there was my Mother Thomasina, though everyone called her Sina. Her two brothers were my Uncle George who was the eldest and my Uncle Joseph who was the baby of the family.

My Uncle George was in the 1914 War and my Mother once told me that he had bayoneted a German Soldier. When he came home from the War there was one time when he had woken up in the middle of the night and standing at the end of the bed was the German soldier he had bayoneted. My Mother said he never slept in that bedroom again. I always thought that it must be a terrible thing: killing someone you don't know and have never seen in your life.

My Dad's Father was Robert Pattison Hymers and his Mother was called Barbara Hymers although her maiden name was Robson. I knew very little about my Grandmother Barbara or the Robsons apart from the fact that my Grandmother Barbara died in her fifties with that dreadful disease, cancer.

The four of us: Alexander, Barbara, me and Norman grew up in a flat with our Mother and Father. The flat consisted of two bedrooms, a living room, which we called the kitchen, and the back kitchen that everyone called the scullery. In the scullery, was the poss-tub where my Mother would do her weekly wash, and in the kitchen was the big fire with an oven attached and a large table where we would eat our meals.

In the front bedroom, was a very large wooden bed. My sister Barbara and I slept at the top of the bed and Alex and Norman slept at the bottom. We were well looked-after when we awoke in the morning, especially if it was a frosty morning. My Mother would warm our clothes on a fire-guard in front of the roaring fire and bring them upstairs for us along with hot water to wash in. We would dress and wash, then we would go downstairs and sit at the big table for breakfast, which was homemade bread that my Mother had baked.

Everyone in the village baked their own bread, new beautiful tasting home-baked bread straight out of the oven. Once it was cooled my Mother would cut slice after slice, great thick doorstops of it spread with lashings of butter and we would eat it with eggs or my Mother would render down pork fat in the oven and then fry the bread in the fat; it was scrumptious and we were all good eaters.

Wages were poor, but we had plenty to eat. I remember a man would come around with his horse and cart selling fresh herring. He'd be dressed in old trousers and a long coat and you could hear the money jingling in his pockets. When she heard him, my Mother would come out of the house carrying a large dish and he would say:

'How many do you want, Mrs Hymers?'

'Tuppence worth,' my Mum would tell him, and he would fill the scale full of herring for two pence.

You'd get about thirty herring for two pence and my Mum would clean them and then bake them.

When they were done, she'd put two on a plate for my young brother, Norman, and two for me, saying: 'Get them down you, they will do you good.'

We were never hungry.

When I was about two, my Mother and I had taken an illness. I remember my Mother saying that Dr Hamilton was sent for and for two months he treated me for an upset stomach. But my Mum said the lady who lived next door to us, Mrs Sawyer, had a different doctor attending her husband, a Dr Harris, and Mrs Sawyers asked the Doctor to attend me too. After Dr Harris had examined me he told my Mother: 'I am sending her to the Fleming Hospital.'

I was in this hospital for three months. They never allowed my Mother or Father to see me. My Mother later told me that my Father had made up a story to tell the Matron, saying that he was going away to work abroad and would be away for a long time, and that way they gave him permission to see me through a glass window. Because he didn't have the money for the bus fare to the hospital my Father walked the seven miles to the hospital, then walked the seven miles back, just so that he could spend five minutes looking at me through a glass window. He'd brought me a honeycomb to eat too although I don't remember eating it.

In those days, if you were very ill or critical as we used to call it, you had a number, and this was placed in the newspaper, on a critical list. I remember my Mother saying my number was on the critical list for one week. But eventually I survived and came home. So that was my hospital adventure.

We had a happy childhood. My Mother didn't work as she had enough to do looking after four children. The man of the house provided for their family. The women looked after their husband's and children and that was more than enough for them to do: all the cooking, washing, cleaning and mending. There weren't any machines to do things for you in those days; you did it all by hand and it was jolly hard work.

My Mother baked all of the time; stoking up the fire to make the oven really hot, she baked blueberry pie apple tarts, chocolate cakes, walnut cakes and coconut cakes. I can smell them now coming out of the oven. My Mother was a great cook!

My Father, Norman Hymers, was an early riser. He was a pattern maker at Harfields factory in Blaydon and he was always at work by seven o'clock in the morning. Any overtime that might going he would also snatch up for the extra money, as there were so many mouths to feed. He'd been in the 1914 war and I remember my Mother saying that he'd lied about his age, as he was only seventeen when he enlisted and you had to be eighteen.

When my Mother was fourteen, she was sent away from home to work as a maid in service at a place called Casterton Hall. Casterton Hall was a school for clergymen's daughters and I remember my Mother saying that they had to rise at five o'clock in the morning and their first job was to scrub the stone floors and light the fires and then set the long tables for the young lady's breakfasts. My Mother said it was very hard work, which I could well imagine. My Aunt Marie, my Mother's oldest sister worked there too. My Mum worked there until she was about twenty-one and then she came home where she met my Dad. My Mum and Dad got married when they were twenty-four and along we all came.

I think I would be about nine years of age when one morning our Mother told us that we were going to be moving house. It was only across the road from our flat. Our new house had been lived in by Mrs Hudson and her husband who was a miner in the Bessie Mine, which was a coal-mine down in Blaydon Burn. There was also another mine in the Burn and the two were known as the Mary and Bessie pits. But Mr and Mrs Hudson were moving to the coal miner's houses in Blaydon Burn so all the Hymers Family moved into 2 Manor Terrace.

Although our new address was 2 Manor Terrace Winlaton, it was known as Cromwell Place, so going back into history Oliver Cromwell must have been around our vicinity somewhere. It was one of four terraced houses. Mr and Mrs Simms lived in number one, our new house was next and then old Mr and Mrs Sawyers were next-door in number 3. Miss Chapman lived in the end house; she looked after her brothers Bob, Mick and Tommy who had been miners in the Mary and Bessie Coal Mines.

The coal-mines were not that far from us and they employed a lot of people. My Father worked at Harfield's in Blaydon but my Grandfather, Sandy Gilfillan and his sons, my Uncles Joseph and George, were all miners and they all lived in the pit-houses down at Blaydon Burn which was where Mr and Mrs Hudson had moved to. We went to bed at about six-thirty at night, but every night we were woken by the trudge of the miner's steel-soled boots as they went to and from their twelve-hour shifts. Their boots on the road just outside of our window: trudge, trudge, trudge.

The new house at Manor Terrace was bigger than the flat we had lived in. We had two bedrooms upstairs, a large kitchen cum living room and also a back kitchen. So now my two brothers slept in the back bedroom and my sister Barbara and I slept in the front bedroom. My Mother's bed was in the kitchen as there was a bed-corner in the space under the stairs. So we all had a place to sleep and everyone was happy.

Chapter 2
Our New House

Out of our new front door was our own small front garden with iron railings and a wrought-iron gate. Down from my Mother's back door and across the fields at the back of our house were three shops. One was a grocery shop that belonged to Mr Sawyers and the shop next to it was Archers Barrels, I remember that the door into Archers had a large sneck on it. If it were windy the door would clash in the wind. There was one time that my Mother was coming through the door when the wind swung it very wide and the large latch smacked hard into my Mother's face. It broke her nose.

The next shop was owned by Mr and Mrs Gibbs. Mrs Gibbs was a lovely fat lady with rosy cheeks and she always wore a mob-cab. They sold groceries and carbide for the coal miners who wore brass lamps on their helmets to light them down the dark coal mines.

Above the shops were two flats. Mr and Mrs Archer lived in one flat and Mr and Mrs Burrell lived in the other one. They all had children the same age as us. Mr Burrell was killed in the War but I am going beyond my story and will come back to that later.

Next to the Gibb's shop was Mr and Mrs Forbes who had one daughter, Lillian. They lived in a stone built house and next to the house was an entrance that in past years had had big wrought iron gates but these must have been taken down at some point and all that was left were the large iron hinges.

We would walk through this entrance into a large backyard where there were two more houses. On the wall as you turned left through the entrance was the cold-water tap, which supplied these houses with fresh clean water. It was always running. We would put our heads under it and drink water. Then we could squirt it and soak our friends. Our clothes were always wet from this but we thought it was great fun.

In the two houses lived Mr and Mrs Bennett and Mr and Mrs Allinson. We were friends with the Bennetts' daughters: Winnie and Evelyn. Opposite the two houses there was a large wash house where the people who lived in the houses would do their washing. If it was raining we would hold concerts in the washhouse and play dress up and have a laugh.

Behind the wash house was a bit of waste ground where Mrs Gibbs would put the large empty carbide barrels. Sometimes there was still a little bit of carbide left in the barrels and we would pour water inside because when the carbide got wet it would start to fizz. We ran away from the barrels as it would swoosh up into the air like an explosion and we used to think it was great fun to make the barrels go swoosh.

There was this one time that we were playing with the carbide barrels and making them go swoosh but this one barrel did not go swoosh! So one of the lads that we knocked around with, he was called Chris, went and looked inside the barrel and as he popped his head over, it suddenly swooshed. Of course, we were laughing but Chris was not. It singed all his hair off, and he had no eyebrows or eyelashes left.

At the far end of the waste ground there was a wall and behind the wall was a large field with horses in it. The owner of the horses was Mr Lowden, who would go around the village with his horse and cart selling fruit and vegetables.

On the left-hand side as you walked out of our back yard were another two houses. Mr and Mrs Howes lived with their son, Maurice, in one house and Maurice's grandparents lived in the other one. As you walked past these houses there was a large stone-built house with big wrought-iron gates and past this were the fields belonging to Robinson's farm. Their two sons, Thomas and Andrew, or Tommie and Andy as we knew them, were tall hefty lads who looked ideal for farm work. My brother Alex was friends with them.

One day, I would have been about four or five,

Alex told my Mum that he was going out with these lads and I said: 'I'm coming too.'

'You're not,' Alex said, and he ran off out of the house so I ran after him until we got to this field where there were cows and I slipped and fell right into a cowpat. I had a white dress on and socks and it was a very soft cowpat so I was covered!

Alex turned to me and said, 'Serves you right for following me.'

I went home thick of cow-shit. My Mum laughed at me, then said, 'Clothes off,' and my Dad put me into the poss-tub full of warm water. It took two lots of water before I was shiny clean again.

Just past the big house with the wrought iron gates there was a winding lane. It was a very dark lane with high walls and was lit by a dim gas lamp. It was known as Lovers' Lane and it was kind of spooky on a night. It was ideal for some of the games we played: kick the block and hide-and-seek.

The Cowens lived on the corner of Lovers' Lane, they were a large family and we all played together. Rena was my age and her sister, Sheila was the same age as my sister Barbara. Next to them lived the Ormstons and then the Boyd's and their son Chris. Chris was the one who got his hair singed by the Carbide swooshing.

As you came out of Lovers Lane and headed back towards my house, on the other side of Sawyers shop were more houses, some with small gardens. Mr and Mrs Chambers and their children, Robert,

Margaret and June lived in the first one but to reach these houses you had to go down some stairs and at the very bottom of them, before you got to the row of houses was a tiny tumbledown cottage where Miss Haig lived. She was very old and dainty and always wore a mob-cab with her hair in a bun underneath it and a long black dress and an apron right down to her ankles. She was a beautiful embroiderer but we were all afraid of her, why I don't know, as I now think that she was a very timid old woman who was very poor. I think that the reason we were so scared of her was that she burnt candles in her house, which is a daft reason to be scared of anyone, but we were only children.

Down the steps and past Miss Haig's house and the Chamber's first house, lived Mr and Mrs Young; they had a large family. Then Mr and Mrs Bilkough with their children Agnes, Jim and Mary and next to them were the Bells and their children Joseph and Mary Bell. Next to them lived Mr and Mrs Hall with their son, Gaynor Hall, who was my elder brother Alex's age. Opposite the Halls was the Aitken family. Their children were called Arnold and John. The Prudhoes lived next-door to them, their children were called Kathleen and Mary, and along from them lived Mr and Mrs Richardson with their daughters Joan, Betty, Margaret and Freda.

I was friends with Joan. She went to Australia with her husband who was a Yugoslavian but her sister Margaret died very young. She had a row with her soldier husband about being late for church and he shot her. Her Mum and Dad were broken hearted.

Mrs Forbes lived in the last house in the row with her children, Kathleen, Sylvia, Sydney and George. So you can see that there were a lot of children around for me to play with and we all used to gather in the big space opposite the terraces to play together.

We played a lot of different games; we would skip, have tops and whips or play statues, which was where you had to stand still, and if you moved you were out. Another game was kick the block. For this game we'd all hide and one person would have to come and look for us; this was the game we played at night when it was dark and really spooky.

There was no traffic in our young life; no cars or busy roads like there are now. People walked or cycled and if anyone bought groceries and they couldn't carry them, out would come the big horse and cart and parcels were put on the cart to be delivered. Off the horse would trot with its brown and white coat and big white fluffy feet and Mr Arthur Watson (who is dead now) would deliver the parcels. So it was very safe to roam around like we did and we did roam far.

So there was a lot to do to fill our time and we enjoyed our lives and were never bored. When we had played our games and were exhausted after using all our energy, our Mothers' would call us in for bedtime, around six thirty at night, as we would normally rise at six thirty in the morning.

Opposite our house on the other side of the road was North Street, which was a long street with more houses. There was a farm there too when I was young; a Mrs Stoke lived there with her family and behind the farm were lovely green fields with more houses below them. The Stokes kept hens and pigs; so they had wire netting to keep the hens and pigs from wandering. Around the back of the farm was a lane with more houses and then on the corner of this lane was a large stone house and a small cottage where Jenny Scott lived with her Father and sisters. There was also the Mary & Bessie club where the young lads would go to play pool. Then there were more fields until you got to the Aerial Flight and the crossroads. This is where the coal mines began.

Chapter 3
Blaydon Burn

If you looked off to the left-hand side of the Aerial Flight you could see the Deputies' homes; these were well built houses that were very smart and we called them the posh houses. The Deputies were the coal mine workers who were like the foremen; they told the miners where to blast and dig for coal.

On the left hand side of the Aerial Flight was the road I was on about which was where the Deputies' Houses were. The name of this road was "The Villas". The Middle Road took you to the old Burn and the mines. There you could see the screen lads and the little pit ponies, they were very hard-worked were those little ponies, they would pull the tubs of coal up from the mines and the screen lads would sort it all out into the different sizes.

As you walked down the Middle Road it led you to the coal-miners' homes at Blaydon Burn But before you got to the miners' houses you could turn off onto the Bessie Steps and a narrow path led you down through the trees to where you could see the pit lines.

My brother Norman and I and all our friends used to follow a path along to the bottom of the Bessie Steps and up to the wood top where you could still see the pit lines. There was a long bridge that the pit engine ran underneath. Steam poured from the spout of the engine. We used to stand on the bridge to get steamed by the engine when it passed and we all thought it was great fun; we used to laugh. When we got to the other side of the bridge we came down the steps onto the pit-heap. The pit-heaps were huge and we'd try to climb them and get our feet and shoes full of muck. Further down was Holby's Dam, which was very deep. All of this was attached to the coal mines.

If you kept on the Middle Road you got to a very steep bank and the long terraced streets of the colliery houses known as Blaydon Burn. Each of the houses had a backyard and in the backyards you would see the miners' clothes dotted here and there on the clotheslines. The pit boots were all cleaned and shined ready for the next shift too. Everything and everyone was kept spotless clean even though mining was a mucky job and there were no washing machines and no baths in the houses. Instead, all of the houses had a large tin bath which was put in the middle of the kitchen floor and filled with hot water from the kettle on the stove.

The miners used to get free coal from the mines,

so their fires were always roaring, and the water from the kettle was really steaming hot when it was poured into the bath. When the miners came back home from work they were jet black so they'd strip off to the waist; boots off, socks off, trousers off only leaving their short trousers on and then they'd kneel on the floor in front of the roaring fire and have a good scrub over the tin bath before they had their dinner. I think they were the cleanest men in Britain.

When we were down the Burn we'd call in for a cup of tea and a homemade rock bun at my Mother's parents; my Granny and Grandpa Gilfillan. They didn't have much money but God love her, my Granny would have given you her last penny. My Granny Gilfillan was always old I thought but hard-working and cooked everything from scratch and my Grandfather Gilfillan was a coal miner and worked hard too.

Friday was pay day for the miners and if I was off school my Gran would ask me to go for my Grandpa's and my Uncle Joseph's pay. Granny would write me a note; I would have the payslips tightly in my hand, and off I would trot, along and down the Bessie Steps to the wood top where I'd see the miners wives standing in a line waiting for their pay. Some of the miners were there too, just finished their shift and all dirty and tired.

I would hand the pay-note from my Granny to the paymaster and he would give me the money and say to me: 'Do not lose it, keep a tight hold on it.'

Once I had the money in my hand, off I'd run back to my Gran's. She'd have my lunch ready when I got back: roast beef and potatoes, cabbage and peas and her Yorkshire puddings were out of this world.

They were good cooks then and I mean they were cooks. You could have a tasty, scrumptious rabbit pie with hock, black pudding and piecrust. After that there was always a pudding: blueberry tart, apple tart, gooseberry. You name it they could make it. Everything homemade. People have lost it now. The roast beef would melt in your mouth and was straight from the farm where they killed their own cattle. My Mother bought her meat from Norman Tweddle the butcher and his cattle grazed in the pastures around the village and were fed with food grown on the farm. Meat wasn't like it is today: fattened with drugs and chemicals. Everything was grown naturally, all the crops, wheat and barley, like it should be. Norman Tweddle had his own pigs too and the animals provided the manure for the crops so that they weren't poisoned with chemicals like they are nowadays.

After I had lunch at my Granny's, I would walk back through the allotment gardens to my home. Coming towards my home were two houses. On the left hand side was a Public House, the Rose and Crown, which was run by Mr and Mrs Pickles. They had two daughters, Ethel and Audrey. I was friends with Ethel. The pub had a large garden at the back. A little further along past the pub and heading towards my house, was a very high wall. Behind this wall was the council stable yard where they kept huge carts and their horses. The council men would take the carts and horses out every Monday when they went to clean out the ash toilets down at the Blaydon Burn pit houses.

The pit houses didn't have flush toilets but instead had earth closets in sheds outside. When you were done, the ash from the coal fires was used to cover up the waste in the toilet.

With six streets of houses down the Burn and about fifteen houses in every street and with every toilet in the street having to be emptied, the horses pulling the ash carts must have got used to standing still while the men got busy with their shovel and cleared all the ash and excrement out of each toilet. It must have been a mucky job to clean them out every Monday.

Chapter 4
School & Play

When we reached the age of five years, we began school. There were three schools: Infant School, the Boys School, and the Girls School. I had reached five years of age and so it was my turn for the Infants: I remember it was a mixed class in the infants. My oldest brother Alex was already in the big Boys School and my sister Barbara was nearing eight years and so she would go into the Girls School.

Our teacher was called Miss Bosenworth. She taught us how to read, write, and do our multiplication tables. Every year we were put into a higher class so we could learn more and by the time we were seven years old we knew our twelve times table. Then at eight I was moved to the Girls School. There were no Boys and Girls mixed. Boys and Girls were kept separate in their own schools and playgrounds. The Boys School was just next door to the Girls School. In the infants, we finished school at three-thirty but in the Big School we finished our day at four o'clock.

I remember one incident that happened at school. It was during our playtime; we had ten minutes playtime morning and afternoon. This young boy, Maurice his name was, ran up to me shouting:

'Mary!'

'Hello Maurice,' I said, 'Where's Norman?'

He said, 'Your Norman cannot come out for his playtime as he been told off by the teacher.'

'What for?' I asked.

Maurice said, 'When we do our sums we are supposed to hand our books to the teacher and get them marked. But your Norman was not getting his sums marked and so the teacher has made him stand in the corner with a bow of ribbon in his hair.'

'Who did this?' I asked.

'Miss Duddy,' he said.

As I walked away from Maurice, I thought: 'Our Norman will really feel silly and he'll cry. I am going home to tell my Mum.'

Then I thought: 'If I don't go back to class they are bound to miss me.'

But I still pelted out of the school yard and I ran all the way down North Street to get back home to tell my Mother.

When I got to our back door, our Mum had the poss-tub out and was doing her weekly wash. She was scrubbing shirt collars, which got really dirty, before she boiled them. My Mum's face was red.

She saw me and said:

'Honey, are you not well?'

Out it came all about what Miss Duddy had done to our Norman.

'She's made him look a fool,' I said.

'Not with my bairn, hinny,' my Mum said, and she left the poss-tub in the yard and went and got her coat, and back up off to the School we went.

When we got to the School, everyone was back inside so my Mum opened up the big wooden door. There was a long hallway and she stood on the inside of the door and shouted down the Hall:

'Where's Babs Duddy?'

The Headmistress came out of her office and all the teachers came out of the staffroom. My Mother opened the door of Miss Duddy's class and I thought she was going to whack her. She got Miss Duddy by the shoulder and said:

'You will make no spectacle of my bairn, Duddy. Six years of age? Is this how you teach bairns?'

I think they had to calm my Mum down. Miss Duddy apologised but my Mum said:

'Norman, honey, get your coat, we are going home.' Then she turned to Miss Duddy and said, 'I will be writing to the Authorities and have you sacked.'

The Headmistress did write to my Mother and Babs Duddy came to see my Mum later to apologise, but this sort of thing did go on in school all the time. You were either the teacher's pet or you were nothing.

Coming home from school at three-thirty on an afternoon, if it was fine, my youngest brother Norman and I would play outside with our friends. There were about twenty of us that all used to live nearby and knock around together.

There was a back yard with grass in-between the houses where my Mother hung her washing. There was a clothes line strung across the grass between the houses and my Mother would hang her washing out with wooden pegs and our clothes would fly in the breeze. In the days before washing machines, washing clothes was all done by hand and the Monday wash was really hard for my Mother.

There was a stone boiler in the back-kitchen with a little fire underneath which was lit every Monday morning. Water was poured into the boiler and heated by the fire.

When the water was boiling, my Mother would get the poss-tub out, fill it with the boiling water from the boiler, and take hold of the poss-stick. She would separate her washing out into whites, then coloureds, then work shirts and socks. It was hard work. The clothes would be possed, scrubbed on a scrubbing board that fitted over the boiler and then put in the boiling water for a good boil. Once they'd been boiled, they were rinsed in clean water then through the old fashioned mangle they would go to wring out all of the water. When all that was done the clean clothes were hung out on the clothes line to dry. That was my Mother's washday.

If it were a hot day our Mother would take the poss-tub outside and fill it with cold-water and three of us managed to step into it and splash around to cool off. My Mum would make cream soda and ginger beer for us to drink. There was no fridge but we did have a pantry off the back-kitchen where there was a great stone slab where you could put things to keep cool. No sunlight got into the pantry so it was always pretty cold in there and everything kept fresh.

As soon as the day was done, we'd come home, put our old clothes on and have our tea which was usually homemade bread and butter. Sometimes too our Mother would have boiled a sheep's head and made broth. After tea, off we'd go to play outside.

When the weather was fine, we'd have our skipping

ropes or we'd play with our tops and whips. In the winter, we each had a sledge, which my Father made for us and when it snowed, we would go and sledge down the big hill of Blaydon Burn where the colliery houses were.

We would wrap up against the cold, wellies over thick socks, our warmest skirt underneath our overcoats and the rest of us wrapped snug in thick jumpers, warm scarves and pixie hood hats.

Down to the Blaydon Burn streets we would go and the Blaydon Burners would come out with their sledges too. The streets were like glass when it snowed and we would sledge down these steep streets right to the bottom. At the bottom of the streets were railings, if there had not been railings then we would have ended up flying over the Battery onto the pit-lines. Sometimes my Mum came out with her neighbour, Ada Forbes, and her two daughters Elsie and Audrey, and they would sledge with us, my Father never did as he was always working.

A Dance With Romeo

Chapter 5
Granny Gilfillan

My Mother couldn't afford new clothes for all of us. Sometimes a lady would come round with lots of second-hand clothes to sell and sometimes my Mum would buy them from her; I think she would call at everyone's house, but really my Mum couldn't afford the second-hand clothes either.

I remember one of our neighbours, Mary Howe, had a husband that worked at Howards. Every year my Mother would buy a Provident cheque off him for twenty pounds. A Provident cheque was like a loan really; you bought a cheque for an amount of money that you paid for in monthly instalments over the year. Twenty pounds was quite a bit of money then. She used to get it near to Christmas time and she'd go to the clothes shops in Newcastle and that way we got new clothes and shoes every year for Christmas.

I remember that one year my Mum bought me a

bottle green jumper suit with red reindeer on it and a pair of ankle-strap shoes that I wore with white socks. She'd buy my brother Norman big heavy boots and my father would put studs on the soles as Norman was heavy on his feet. Norman also got short trousers, thick knee-length socks, jumpers and shirts. Our new clothes were always put away for Christmas. My Mum did without for us; she was lucky if she got a new pinny for herself.

Friday night was bath night. A large tin bath would appear in front of the roaring large fire in the kitchen and there we would have our weekly bath. We washed every night before we went to bed: face, ears, neck, legs and arms. But Friday night was when we had a good scrub-down and washed our hair.

Sunday night was special. We used to go down to my Gran's to keep her company. The lamps on the street were lit by gas and showed a very poor light and my sister Barbara, my cousin Peggy, Norman and I would walk down by the Gun Huts past the Miners' allotments to Blaydon Burn. It was spooky and really we were frightened, but it was all an adventure.

There were quite a few Gilfillans in Winlaton. One of the Gilfillans, my Great-Grandfather, was a keen sword-dancer. I didn't know my Great-Grandfather but there was a large photograph of him on my old Granny's sideboard. It was a great long solid wooden sideboard with a huge photograph of my Great-Grandfather with his long bushy beard and cap stuck on the top of head. My Mother said his name was Robert and he married a girl called Mary Doyle, my Great-Grandmother, who was an Irish lady. I have her photograph now and her hands look very gnarled and worn. My Mother said she had a heart of gold and would go around the village helping to deliver babies.

My Mother had a hard childhood. My old Granny was kind but it was a big family and with only one wage times were hard and sometimes my Mother and her sisters could not go to school, as they could not afford shoes.

My Grandfather, Alexander Gilfillan, was the breadwinner. He was about six foot two inches tall but some of the coal seams were only eighteen inches high and miners like my Grandfather had to crawl on their bellies in the pitch black and dirty cold water for twelve hours a day.

I often heard my Mother say that my Grandpa would come back tipsy on a Saturday night and be very arguesome. I think that he was very strict and what he said was law. My Mother hated drink and I think this was because of my Grandfather.

My Uncle Joe was my Mother's youngest brother. My Mum said that a man used to come round with a horse and cart and my Gran used to buy her groceries from him. The man's name was Woodger and whenever my Uncle Joe saw him, he would laugh and say: 'Here's Woodger for the furniture,' and they would all laugh as well but that was close to the truth.

When they reached the age of fourteen my Mother and her sister, my Aunt Marie, had to go away to work at Casterton Hall in Cumbria. Casterton Hall was a school for Rector's daughters and it was a big place so it was hard work. My Aunt Isabel was allowed to stay at home; my Mum said that she helped my Gran in the house and also did dressmaking.

The women in those days kept their homes spotless. That was their job. Their back-kitchens were scrubbed daily, as were the outside steps and the majority of them had stone floors made of sandy stone from the local quarry so keeping them clean was hard work.

When their husbands, the miners, came back from a shift their pit-boots were scraped with a sharp knife as the small studs in the soles were full of muck from the pit. Their boots were then cleaned and polished and hung on the clothesline and their trousers washed, dried and mended. Everything was cleaned and gleamed for the next shift.

When they came from work, the table was already set for dinner. The miners would get washed and then they would eat. I've seen my Grandfather's plate heaped high like a mountain and he could shift it. I've heard my Mother say that some of the miners used to complain that he worked too hard.

They were strong men though. I remember one story where my Grandfather Gilfillan was troubled with an ulcerated stomach and so he was sent to the Royal Victoria Hospital where they told him that he needed to go through an operation. But the night before he was due to be operated, he put his clothes on and walked seven miles from Newcastle back to Winlaton. He told my Mum: 'They are not cutting me,' and he lived to be eighty-six years old.

When we arrived at my Gran's, we would pull our chairs around the roaring coal fire in the kitchen and she would tell us stories of when she lived at Stephen Hall in Stella.

It was lovely to be sitting around the fire, especially on a cold and frosty night. The moon would be shining, the stars twinkling and there would be frost patterns on my Gran's windows. We were warm and cosy and my, they were spectacular, the patterns on the windows.

Stephen Hall was a desolate place. It was all farms and fields with a sand quarry on one side and in the eighteen hundreds it had been a convent. But when my Gran was younger, she lived there with my Grandfather and this is where my Mother, Aunt Marie, Aunt Isabel, Uncle George, and Uncle Joseph were born.

So my Gran would tell her stories of Stephen Hall. Late at night, she said, she would fill her coal scuttle for her fire the next morning and one night as she was filling the scuttle she looked up and there was a nun standing beside her. She said that as she saw the nun there were shining lights all around her and then the nun disappeared. After that she said, she often saw this nun appear.

There was one time, she told us, that she used

to go every week to her sister, Sarah, who lived in Blaydon. Her sister was very ill so my Gran would walk down the pit line to collect her sister's washing and do it for her. It was a pretty rough trek down the pit line, about three miles each way and rough woodland on either side. To get there my Gran had to pass the German Ovens and the Tar Works, which were all connected with the coal mines. This was where we used to go down to the coal mines and cross the Butterfly Bridge to get steamed from the pit-engine.

As you walked down towards Blaydon Burn, passing the Rose and Crown Public House, there were a lot of garden allotments. My Dad and a lot of the miners had their own plots where they grew vegetables. The straight way down was past the garden allotments but before that was another way that took you through the Gun Huts. We used to take this route and it brought us through the fields where you could really smell the Tar Works beside the coal mines; we called these fields the Hot Springs. The smell had something to do with benzene from the tar works. The Tar Works had big chimneys with smoke coming out of them and when you looked at them, they looked like they were shaped like a man so of course we called it the Iron Man.

By nine o'clock at night my Gran would be making her way back home after picking up the washing from her sister's. It was pitch-black coming back as there weren't any street lights. On her way home one moonlit night she told us that she saw this man swinging on a creaky iron farm gate. My Gran said to him: 'Geordie, you gave me the fright of my life!'

Next day my Gran was doing her washing out in the back yard and mentioned to her neighbour that Geordie had given her a fright by swinging on the farm gate the night before. Her neighbour then told her that Geordie had hung himself in the old barn the day before, so she told us: 'I must have seen Geordie's ghost on the gate.'

My Gran had two doves that would come to her front door and my Gran would feed them. I have heard my Mother say my Gran had a baby, and it was in its cot, and the two doves flew in, perched on the end of the cot and put their little heads under their wings. When my Gran went to the cot the baby was dead. This was before my Mother was born.

So we'd sit at the fire while my Gran told us her stories until it was time to come home and we were well and truly spooked. It was pretty dark outside and we walked at first through to the Gun Huts. Then we started to walk a bit quicker, then we would all begin to run, especially my brother Norman who was a better runner than me. So I was left behind and there was a fight when we got home. My Mother would laugh at us and say: 'Has your Gran spooked you?' We were terrified but we enjoyed the fear, the excitement, the running home, the whole adventure and so of course we went back every Sunday to keep my Gran company.

Chapter 6
My Father's Family

My Father was in the nineteen fourteen war; he was only seventeen when he joined but he told them he was eighteen. He told us that the only reason he'd enlisted was because all of his brothers had been called up so he thought he'd join too. I remember him telling us that during the War he was a medic on a hospital ship that ferried wounded troops between the Dardanelles and Alexandria during the Gallipoli campaign.

My Dad had five brothers and two sisters. My Father's brothers were my Uncle Robert Pattinson Hymers, my Uncle Joseph Hymers, my Uncle Robson and then came my Father Norman followed by two younger brothers, my Uncle Douglas and my Uncle Albert who was a priest in a church. Uncle Albert was the youngest of the brothers and he died young at the age of forty-five.

They all attended church, and I still have my pa's

Communion Prayer book. All of the brothers were engineers and blacksmiths; my Father had served his time as a pattern maker and my Uncle Albert was a priest. He was called up for duty in the First World War but he never believed in shooting the enemy, he was a conscientious objector. This was his belief and he stuck to it.

My grandmother's name was Barbara Lithgow Hymers and my sister Barbara was called after her. My Father also had two younger sisters, my Aunties Ena and Doris. My Aunt Ena and my Uncle Albert never married but my Father's brothers all had families, and when they had a son they would name them after their Father Robert Hymers.

My Grandfather Robert Hymers was known as Bob and he was the manager of the main hotel in Blaydon, the Station Hotel. On a Friday night when everyone got their pay packet some of the men would call into the pub for a drink on their way home from work. My Grandfather would say to them: 'Go home with your wages to your wife and then I'll serve you what you want when you come back.'

My Father helped his Father in the cellar with the barrels of beer and he served in the bar too. None of the sons drank apart from my Father; I think my Father was the only one who liked a drink.

The Hymers were related to Smith Patterson's, the foundry and engineering works at Blaydon, and going back there's a lot of history to the Hymers. There was a Hymers Court at Gateshead, a Lord

Mayor in the eighteen hundreds and a Hymers College as well.

Chapter 7
Winlaton Village

I never got round to telling you about our village where I grew up. Winlaton had one main street, which was called Front Street. The Highlander pub was the first thing on Front Street with the Post Office next to it. Then there was another pub and opposite that was Mary Martins Paper Shop with George Gilfillan's shop next to that. After Gilfillan's was the butcher's, Walter Rehy, which had rabbits hanging on hooks outside the shop window and Harold's sweet shop.

Opposite my Grans favourite shop; Walter Wilsons, which was where she bought her cooked ham, was Hardy's fish shop. Then there were some houses, their toilets were in the back yards. After the houses was another big Inn and Walkers cake shop. A small opening led you onto Parliament Street, where my friend Elsie lived and Jimmy and Betty Temple, and then Glendinning the Undertaker.

I was good friends with Elsie Jennings and we went everywhere together. On Monday nights I would walk up to the village to call on her and together we went to learn tap dancing. It was at the YMCA and our dance teacher was called Miss Milligan. The YMCA was a big wooden hut and dances held there too. I loved dancing. This got me into trouble. I was being confirmed at St Pauls Church and our tap-dancing lesson was every Monday night, but I'd been told by the Rector that every Monday night we had to go to the Rectory to learn our catechism for our Confirmation. Well Monday night came and Mary was missing from catechism, but not from tap-dancing. So the Rector came to my Mother and said:

'Mary is always missing and I want her to come to the Rectory to learn her prayers.'

So I went to the Rectory the next Monday and I got a jolly good telling off from the Rector, but I was confirmed eventually.

We used to run messages for my Mother. My Mum would say: 'Go to the Co-Op store,' and I would take a note to the shop.

There were two sides to the Co-Op, one side for butter and bacon and tins, the other side of the shop was where you bought your groceries. I'd give my note to Harry at the Co-Op and I'd be proud. Harry would take the note and if there was no butter on the stand he would go into the back-shop and bring out a wooden barrel. It had three wooden hoops around and he'd get his little claw hammer on the hoops and the barrel would come apart. Then with a sharp knife, he'd cut three pounds of best butter: my Mother always gave us butter on our bread. Then I'd ask for about three pounds of bacon. It was all neatly wrapped in brown paper and then we'd go to the other side of the Co-Op for our two stone of flour, yeast and sugar. That was neatly wrapped too and off I'd go home, having done my good deed for the day.

From time to time a neighbour would knock on my Mothers door and they would ask: 'Sina, would you like a load of pit coal?' Every month without fail, anyone who worked for the Mines received a ton of coal. So, if they had plenty in their coal-house during the summer, they'd knock on my Mum's door and ask if she wanted to buy it. Of course, my Mum would jump at the chance. She had two tin buckets and the coal was around Lovers Lane, which was about a five-minute walk away. God love her, if it was a warm day, you'd see the sweat drip off my Mum, as she shovelled and carried a ton of coal back to our coal house, two buckets at a time. But she was glad of it, as it meant that we would have plenty of coal and be toasty warm in the winter. My Father was always at work so he couldn't help her carry any of it. But I remember that he did help my Mother to bake the bread when she was busy with other things.

My Mum began her housework at 6 o'clock in the morning and she'd work until midnight. The washing was something else: boiling the clothes, scrubbing them in the washtub, and then pushing them through the mangle. Then she'd cook, to make sure that we were always full of food.

I remember my Mother's favourite butcher; Norman Tweddle used to say to my Mum: 'Sina I'm killing some cattle tomorrow, bring an enamel pail and I'll give you some blood' and my Mum would bring her pail up the butchers and get it filled with blood. She used the blood to make black pudding and you've never tasted anything like my Mums black pudding. She would cut a chunk off for Norman and I to eat while it was still steaming hot and we would munch away on it.

As well as the washing and cooking, there was the cleaning. Black-leading the stove and scrubbing and whitening the steps and floors, as well as all of the usual dusting and floor sweeping and washing. My Mother never put her feet up. Even when she was sitting down, she was busy with something. My Father had made her frames for making her own rugs. We had strips of oilcloth on the floor around the edges of the room but oilcloth was expensive and we couldn't afford to cover the whole floor with it. Instead, my Mum made her own Hooky and Proggy mats from our old clothes. She'd buy Hessian or use old flour sacks from the bakers to back the rugs with.

The Hessian was sewn on the mat frames and a pattern would be drawn on it. Then the old clothes; old coats and woollen dresses were cut into long thin strips, and my Mother would use her hook to either pull or push the strips of cloth through the Hessian.

Proggy mats were made when she pushed the strips through the Hessian and Hooky mats were when she'd hook the fabric up through the material. I remember one rug she made of roses and leaves, where she used green for the leaves and different colours for the roses. When the rug was finished, it was pretty. It had a black border and roses in the middle. It was a fireside rug and with it being new, we would sit and admire my Mother's work.

We had no money, but we sure never got bored with life. We made our own fun and we were happy and always found something to do.

Guy Fawkes was a day to remember. We had our big bonfires and my brother, Norman, would be dressed in a dress, with lipstick on and a lovely bonnet on his head and our friend Bobby Simms who lived next door was dressed the same. Norman and Bobby would go round the village, knocking on people's doors saying, 'Penny for the Guy' and they would have this rag doll all dressed up. We bought crackers too. The bonfire was lit and the crackers set alight and we watched each other's fireworks.

My brother, Norman, and I, and all our childhood friends, all knocked around together. We would travel down to the Aerial Flight where the crossroads were and go down the old Burn. We would watch the pit-lads working with their small tubs of coal and the small pit ponies pulling the tubs. They were strong little horses and they worked jolly hard. On a Sunday, the pit ponies had the day off and got to roam the fields. My brother Norman and his good friend Joe Pringle, who he went to school with, would ride the pit ponies in the fields.

My brother's friend Joe Pringle lived in Rectory Lane. There were many houses there and it was next to St Paul's Church, where they rang the church bells on a Sunday. We were made to go to church every week and it was lovely to hear them as we walked up to the Church. To get to Rectory Lane we had to walk through the village of Winlaton and at the top of Rectory Lane was a blacksmiths shop and my brother, Norman, and Joe Pringle would watch Geordie the blacksmith shoe his horses. They were fascinated by this. Geordie the Blacksmith would make and fix farm equipment too, as well as other things. Along by Geordie's Blacksmiths shop were fields and a path; they called this the Half-Fields Road, which led down to Winlaton Mill.

It was all woodland down there and there were lovely green fields and a river where we would paddle, with a bridge and few whitewashed cottages. My friend, Elsie, had a crush on one of the lads we used to knock about with. She only ever had eyes for this young man, Bobby Surrey, who she married later on. She does not live far from where I live now and today, as I write this, I'm looking out of my window and I have watched her funeral go by to the crematorium. All those happy years have gone and the lovely memories. Happy times. At least we thought so.

One of the good times we had was the Winlaton Hoppings. This happened every Easter. Winlaton was noted for having a great Hoppings and it was a huge affair. People came from far and near to go to it: Ryton, Whickham, Scotswood, they came from all over. The Hoppings set up on Hood Square in the village. There were a lot of rides: the Noah's Ark, Waltzers, the stalls, the Flying Chairs, the Big Boats where everyone screamed, the Dive Bomber, we went on that and we did scream!

We used to go to the Hoppings on a Saturday night with our Mum and Dad and we'd get all dressed up in our new clothes. I was in my new red blazer, my rosebud dress and my white socks with ankle-straps. Our Norman wore his new long trousers, new shoes, white shirt, tie and jacket, with his hair pasted with Brylcreem. We'd have a try on all the rides and on the stalls too, and we'd watch the shows as well. On the Sunday morning, there'd be a big parade with bands, and everyone turned out to see this great display. There were thousands there and everyone had an open house, everyone was friendly.

We had a great childhood. Of course, we did as we were told, but we were free to do as we wanted to do and our parents did their best for us. I had a great Father, he never lost his temper. My Mother was always busy, but always had time to make us cream soda or ginger beer, she was a dab hand at everything.

When my brother, Norman, was eight years old he took diphtheria. In those days, if you got diphtheria, the house was fumigated and we were quarantined and could not go to school for a few weeks, as diphtheria was contagious. The doctor was called and Norman was taken to Norman's Riding Hospital. Normans Riding was an isolation hospital on the outside of Winlaton. It specialised in TB cures and was a good twenty minutes walk away from my house, well past our schools and into the countryside. Norman stayed there for about six weeks.

When he came out of hospital, I contracted a germ in my throat. I was sent back and forward to the Royal Victoria Infirmary, every other week, until they decided to take my tonsils out. I was in hospital for one week. I remember the Matron wore a spotless clean cap perched upon her head. It was white. Her uniform was meticulously clean. It was a navy and white striped dress, with long sleeves and white starched cuffs and aprons. The Matron gave the orders to her staff, and the nurses jumped to attention. Under the Matron, there was a Sister and then the nurses, who looked after the long wards with their polished floors. There were about thirty beds in the ward. This time my Mum and Dad were able to come and see me. After my tonsils were out, I never had a sore throat again.

Although we didn't have much money, my Mother and Father did their best for us. We were happy and we always had a good Christmas. As well as our new clothes, my Father made sure that we always got a little present. We used to get a Savings card from Sawyers Grocery Shop and the Grocer, Mr Sawyers, would mark the card for each penny we saved through the year. It was hard trying to get even one penny on the card, but we managed until we had a shilling saved up. Then on Christmas Eve, we would buy our selection box of chocolates and they would be taken from us until Christmas Day came.

My Mother would make her own Christmas tree. She'd ask the Grocer for two wooden hoops from the butter barrels that the butter came in and she'd push one hoop into the middle of the other. Then she'd buy crepe paper and she'd crumple it and crimp it all around the hoops and hang Christmas toys from it. It was beautiful by the time she'd finished with it. When the house was decorated and the fire crackling we would go to bed. We always woke up early on Christmas morning. We all got apples and oranges and chocolates, and my Father made toys for the boys; he made our Norman a wooden steam engine. The boys were always bought a meccano set as well. The girls got clothes: slippers, pleated skirts and ankle-strap shoes that my Mother had bought with the Provident Cheque and I'd get all dolled up in my new clothes

My Mother always bought a joint of pork for Christmas dinner, which we'd eat with steamed and baked potatoes, Brussels sprouts, peas and Yorkshire puddings, and after that we'd have Christmas Pudding and custard.

For tea, we'd have Christmas Cake with marzipan, and icing with silver beads and Merry Christmas piped in icing on the top. My Mother would have also made date tarts and cheese scones and walnut cake and coconut cake, and we'd eat until we were really stuffed and could not move.

Chapter 8
A Rumour of War

I was thirteen years old and there was many a rumour about a war with Germany going on. We had a radio and my Mother and Father would turn on the radio for news. What was happening? I remember Mr Chamberlain, the Prime Minister, had gone to Germany to see the German Chancellor and he came back and was pleased to announce on the radio that there was going to be peace. I think that everyone breathed a sigh of relief. However a few months went by and Adolf Hitler, the German Chancellor, invaded Poland and of course that brought England into the War.

When War was declared it completely changed our lives. I was still at school but my sister Barbara had just left, and to help the War Effort she and her friend decided to become nurses. So they were told to go to Preston to be trained in a hospital and off they went.

My Mum laughed and said, 'I'll give her a week.'

'Do you think so?' I said.

My Mother said: 'Honey, Barbara will not like that work but good luck to her if she can stick it out, it's an interesting career and a good one, but you have to be dedicated.'

Two weeks went by and sure enough, my Mother received a letter from my sister Barbara saying: 'Coming home Mum.'

My Mum and I went into Newcastle Station to welcome her home. With the war on there were many men receiving their call-up papers to join the forces and fight in the war. Everything was all hustle and bustle and Newcastle Central Station was crammed with troops. We managed to squeeze through to meet the train and there was Barbara with her case. We gave each other a hug and she said, 'I couldn't stick it, Mum.'

Barbara told us that she'd had to run a message and she passed the mortuary and that was the thing that changed her mind as the mortuary was dark and she was frightened. But my Mum just said: 'Never mind, you'll soon get another job,' and that was that.

My sister signed on the dole but quickly got a job on the munitions. It was hard work as they had to do twelve-hour shifts but the money was good.

Barbara worked all of the War at Armstrong's Munitions. It was a huge factory. A few thousand worked there. The factory buildings started at

Scotswood Road on the edge of the Tyne and went right along to Elswick at the start of Newcastle some three miles away. I think the Germans tried very hard to hit it with their bombs but they never managed to. A three-mile- long factory and they missed it every time.

My sister worked a twelve-hour day shift for two weeks and then two weeks night shift. Good money. When their shift was finished, out came the thousands from the factory. The trams and buses running from Newcastle to Scotswood were crammed. They were so full, passengers were standing on the steps, hanging onto the doors, upstairs and downstairs were packed like sardines in a tin. Trams were full. Buses were full. Trains were full. England was in full swing.

When the War started my brother Alex was about seventeen and working in the filthy coal mines. I knew he hated his job and that he had been good at mathematics at school, top of his class. As soon as War was declared Alex saw it as a chance to get out of the mines and he and a friend volunteered for the Navy. He passed the exams and was all ready to sign up for the twelve years but when he told my Mother and Father what he'd done my Father said: 'You did what?' and my Mother said: 'I'm not letting you go for twelve years.'

With him being only seventeen and underage, my parents could stop him from going and they did. So his naval career fell through and instead he joined the Air Force and was stationed at Church Fenton in North Yorkshire. He joined to be an Air Gunner till my Mother put her foot down and told him: 'You go back there and you will have a choice to be something else.'

I think that Alex changed his mind after the air raids in Germany as well, as it was the Air Gunner who was the one on the floor riddled with bullets. Instead, he qualified as a navigator and was posted to Burma.

War had broken out and life really began. Everyone was war crazy. There was a Fireman, the Home Guard and Wardens. My Mother along with every woman in the village had to buy material, preferably black and make curtains for the black out. There was not a chink of light allowed out of anyone's window. If there was then there was a loud knock on your door and the Warden would say: 'Mrs Hymers I can see a light through your window.'

There was voluntary work for the ladies putting together the gas masks; my Mother volunteered for that. Everyone had a gas mask and we had to carry these everywhere. They came in three different sizes: small, medium, and large. The schools were closed down for a while; of course, this was great when you were thirteen years old – no school!

There was rationing and we were all issued with ration books. Each person was allowed so much butter, sugar, flour, bread and meat. Chocolate was rationed too but we used to give our chocolate rations to the younger children. If there were eggs, you'd have to stand in a queue and it would be a mile long so you had to be patient. I've seen my Mother stand for hours. There wasn't much of anything but my Mother was a great cook and we'd eat a lot of big dinners; stews and broths, so we never went hungry. If Mrs Robson killed a pig, she kept pigs in a large allotment she had and would occasionally kill one, then my Mother would buy pork from her although this was against the rules.

Every family was issued with an air-raid shelter to protect us from the bombs dropping. It was a corrugated shelter made of thick metal with curved sides that fitted together. We all had to dig in the earth to help my Dad to bury the shelter to make it safe. My brothers and my Dad did most of the digging; they dug right into the earth because the further down you dug, the better.

When the shelter was built, it was covered in old sandbags and square pieces of turf were put on the roof so that it was well protected. My Father made bunk beds to put into the shelter and we put old blankets and rugs in as well to make it cosy. An oil lamp kept us warm. We had to keep heating the shelter because when it got cold it was very damp.

I remember that our next-door neighbour, Mrs Simm, was given a large shelter but they had to share it with Mr and Mrs Foster and their daughter, Alice, who had moved in next door. Old Mr and Mrs Sawyers who had lived next to us had died.

Our beautiful iron railings and front gate were taken away to help with the war. Even the cemetery railings and gate opposite the church of St Paul's were taken to help the war effort.

Our small village of Winlaton was turned into a barracks. The people who lived in the big house with the wrought iron gates were moved into a new home. The farmhouse where my brother Alex was friends with the farm lads, Andrew and Johnny, that was empty too; they'd been moved to another farm at Greenside.

The soldiers poured into Winlaton. There were army wagons in the farm below where we lived. The Hallgarth House was filled with troops. The big house below where we lived was filled with officers. The inn at the top of the village next to Armstrong's shop was full of soldiers. Further down from the cemetery next to our school was the Church Hall. It was great for dances but the soldiers ate there too; breakfast lunch, tea and supper were all served there.

It wasn't only the men who went to war, for women there was the ATS Army, the WAAF, which was where my brother Alex met his wife, and the Wrens. They all played a great part in the 1940 war. And all of the countries! There was Canada, Australia, New Zealand and Britain.

This man from Germany, Hitler, was trying to conquer the world and we had to stop him. We had a great Prime Minister, Winston Churchill, and Roosevelt and Stalin who all knew what they were doing. I think Churchill was the best Prime Minister that we ever had. But we stood alone for a long time; until the Japs bombed Pearl Harbour and Germany invaded Russia; that was how the Yanks and the Russians got into our war.

So that was my sister Barbara on the 'Munitions and my brother Alex in the Air Force and Winlaton was alive. I had reached the age of fourteen and had left school with little facts in my head but I'd got a job working at John Sinclair's cigarette factory. It paid good money. Everyone smoked. Soldiers, miners, everyone including me but my Mother condemned smoking; we were not allowed to smoke, so we had to smoke sneaky. It was difficult because even before I got home my Mother would smell the smoke. So my sister and I would eat scented sweets, Parma Violets, and scented cashews, to take the smell away but Mum could still tell and we'd get a good telling off. My Mum was the boss not my Pa; he was quiet and wouldn't say boo to a goose.

Our boss, Mr Sinclair, was good to the girls who worked for him. There were about a thousand girls and twice a year we'd get a nice fat bonus. My Mother was always pleased with this and I always got a posh rig out: coat, dress, shoes, the lot. We all thought we were quite grown up at fourteen years old.

Chapter 9
The Wars Still Going On

I'm fifteen years old and the War's still going on. I was working at John Sinclair's cigarette factory and as soon as I got home from work I'd put my lipstick and earrings on and change into something magic and be transformed into a good looking girl in a dance dress and dance shoes.

Fabric was rationed but we still managed to dress nicely. My Mother made sure that my sister and I were always very smart, all the girls were. We all always wore lipstick and powder and we never wore trousers. My parents used to save up their clothing ration coupons and give them to us so that we could have new clothes. I had some nice clothes. You could buy a lovely costume with a flare at the bottom of your jacket and pleated skirt.

I remember one dress my Mum bought me: turquoise taffeta with yards of material in the skirt. I wore it with black suede court shoes and big-hooped gypsy earrings. She bought me a chocolate brown coat with half a belt at the back as well and a pinafore dress with a chiffon blouse with bishops sleeves. It was emerald green.

If your hair was long, like mine was, you wore it in a snood. A snood was like a fishermen's net that caught your hair at the back. We'd buy sequins, emerald green, pink on gold and silver and sew them onto the snoods so that they were very dressy. Sometimes we'd put roses in our hair too.

I am afraid, I was dance mad. So was my sister when she was on day shift. We would go to the Miners' Dance in Winlaton. It was quite a nice dance hall with a lovely sprung floor. Then there was the big YMCA hut where the soldiers had their breakfast, lunch and tea. These soldiers had their own dance band and in this big hut where they ate they held two dances a week.

I was really good at dancing and the Army band was a pretty good band. There were five soldiers in the band and we would foxtrot, tango and rhumba away until the last waltz played at eleven o'clock. The last waltz played was usually "Who's Taking You Home Tonight After The Dance Is Through."

All the soldiers would go to the dances and everyone from the village went too, including the Mums, my Mother as well. I've seen my Mother all dressed up to go to the dance; she was more like a big sister than a Mum, and we had no secrets. My sister would go with her friends and I would go with my Mum.

Once I remember the Hall was full and I mean really full. Because it was a small village everyone knew everyone, and there was one lady, she was quite large, called Mrs Skidmore. She was a big jolly woman. Mrs Skidmore decided to go to the toilets and when she came out her dress was tucked into her knickers, well they were more like pantaloons really. She walked right from the top of the dance hall all the way down into the middle and there was her skirt tucked into her knickers at the back. Everyone was laughing and shouting: 'Mrs Skidmore, your bloomers are showing!'

But Mrs Skidmore just laughed and shouted back to us: 'I don't know what you're all looking at, everyone's got an arse!'

If we weren't off dancing then we'd go to see a film. The pictures would be filled with rows of soldiers. There would be some young lads from the village amongst them but most of them would be soldiers and they'd all have a girl sitting beside them. Some of the soldiers were no older than nineteen. My sister's boyfriends were older but not by much, they were about twenty-three or twenty-four. You felt safe with them all around you, especially when the sirens roared and the searchlights came out, and you could hear the Boom! Boom! of the guns.

Everyone opened their doors to the soldiers and was kind to them. I have seen about thirty soldiers in my Mum's house. They were all decent young lads. You could walk home from a dance or a film late at night and you never heard of rape or murder or stabbings.

I had crush on one solider. His name was Vaughn Thomas. He came from Wales. He was nineteen years old and we were good friends but he never took me out. I was a bit wary of going out with boys. At fifteen years old, I was too young. I would dance with them, but although I was asked a few times I would never let them take me home. I always thought: 'Here today and gone tomorrow.' It never dawned on me to go out with them.

However, my sister, Barbara, who was eighteen was always seeing someone and had many boyfriends. She would set a lot of dates on with soldiers; sometimes she showed up for the dates and sometimes she didn't. The first boyfriend she had was Reg Funnel and he was madly in love with my sister. She went out with Reg for three months when he was stationed in Winlaton.

They were the first lot of the Royal Fusiliers, the Border lads, and their Army Wagons were in the fields opposite our home. When they had done their training in Winlaton they were shipped abroad to do their job in the War. All the village girls had soldier boyfriends and when the time came for them to go abroad, there was much crying and many broken hearts. Then Winlaton was quiet for two weeks until another batch of soldiers came in.

There was this one time that my sister Barbara wrote to this lonely soldier; he was her penfriend. If the soldiers wanted a penfriend then, before they were shipped out of the Barracks, they would write their name and address on the wall above their beds. We would copy the addresses off the Barrack walls when they had gone and the girls would write to them.

One night there was a knock at the door and so I went to see who it was. A blonde soldier was stood there and he asked if Barbara Hymers lived here. Of course I told him that, yes she did.

The soldier was in hospital blue, he had been wounded, and his arm was in a sling. He was limping too and he had a walking stick.

My Mum was making tea at the time, sausage, chips and egg. I brought the soldier in and he introduced himself as Barbara's penfriend. My sister's face was a picture; I think she wrote to him but never thought to see him. So, Barbara was aghast but I thought it was really funny. We were all seated around the table, my Mum, my Pa, Norman, Barbara and now of course the soldier. Then there was me, giddy Mary.

The soldier ate his chips and then he looked at my sister Barbara and said:

'Would you cut my sausage Barbara?'

I dived under the table and had to stick a hanky in my mouth to stop laughing. Our Barbara stuck her head under the table to see what I was doing and saw me laughing and she was ready to laugh too but we had to control our giggles so we didn't embarrass the poor lad. He had been wounded in France and was in the RVI hospital in Newcastle for his wounds. God love him, we never saw him again.

We'd sometimes pop over to the Dance at Greenside as well, there would usually be about four of us. We'd get the bus there but we'd walk the two and half miles back afterwards, through Barlow and along the top of the Sandy Banks near to the quarry. If the sirens went then it was quite spooky walking Sandy Banks as there were very few houses. You could hear the guns and the drone of the aeroplanes and we'd run until we reached the old barn and more houses.

We had hectic nights. You'd be fast asleep in your bed, in a deep sleep and then at about 2 or 3 in the morning you heard the wail of the sirens. My Father never let us get out of bed until he heard the big guns stationed along the coastline some thirty miles away. You could really hear them booming. So when my Father heard these he'd call us and make us get out of bed and of course we did. I don't know when my Dad ever slept during the War.

We'd get dressed, collect the dog and the budgie, and make our way to the air-raid shelter. You could hear the drone of the aeroplanes as they tried to bomb Armstrong's Munitions factory where my sister worked which was three miles away.

We were supposed to stay in the shelter, but of course, outside we would go to watch the searchlights. It was inky black outside, not a chink of light anywhere but the searchlights lit the heavens. They would swing around and light up the sky and then you saw the bombers dropping flares, and when they dropped incendiaries that made the place much lighter.

When it got too bad, into the shelter we would go. You'd hear this screeching and whistling. When you heard that it meant the bomb was sure coming down and you were thinking, 'Is it going to hit?' Down it came. It missed everyone. Next day you would see that everyone's windows had been blown out. I remember that there was a young girl Doris, who was my sister's friend, she said she was coming down the stairs when a bomb dropped nearby and the blast from the bomb blew her front door clean off its hinges and it fell on her head and knocked her out.

One thing about the Army, they came round afterwards to see everyone was all right. There'd be glass all over, wires and cables down. No sleep that night but whatever had happened during the night, we started work religiously at eight o clock every morning and worked until five pm. I think that Armstrong's, the Munitions factory where my sister worked, was the main target but they never succeeded in bombing it. They tried a few times but it was on the winding River Tyne and so it was awkward to hit.

All the soldiers would come into our house and my Mum would do the officers' washing. I remember one officer that used to visit a lot; his name was Daphne. He was very young; I think he looked about twenty-one, and he was gorgeous. Everyone fell in love with him. Many's the time I would be coming home from work and I would see my Father going for a walk.

'Where's Mum?' I'd ask and my Dad would reply:

'She's making tea for the battalion so I've come out for a walk.'

Sure enough when I'd get home, you'd not be able to move for squaddies.

Chapter 10
2 Years & Getting Complicated

The war had been going on for two years now and it was getting complicated. There had been Dunkirk and lots of our lads were lost. I knew one or two Winlaton lads who had been killed there. The soldiers who dated my sister Barbara would walk her home and then come into my Mother's for a cup of tea and a sandwich. They'd tell my Mother that they only had two or three weeks left in Winlaton and they thought they'd be sent abroad. So, that's how we found out what was happening.

My brother Alex had been in Burma for a year. He'd been stationed at Church Fenton before he was sent to Burma and while he was there he'd got engaged and then married to a young lady called Jean who was in the WAAF.

While the War rolled on, we got on with our lives. Sometimes we'd go to the Blaydon Pictures; there was the Plaza, the Pavilion and the Empire. If you went to the Empire it was near the railway station and when the trains passed the seats would shake and you'd hear the trains whistle. Newcastle was full of soldiers: Yanks, Canadians, Australians and British. It was a giggle because as you came down Clayton Street you'd see some Yanks and they'd whistle after you and shout: 'See yah tonight!'

We worked shifts from eight o'clock in the morning with a one-hour lunch-break. After lunch we'd go back to work until five pm and home-time and a mad dash for our bus.

The Winlaton Bus Service belonged to Hurst and there would be five buses on and they'd all be full of workers. Marlborough Crescent was where the buses came in and stopped and all of the bus stands would be filled with buses and people. All of the unmarried women worked full-time, there were no part-time workers and there was plenty of work for everyone.

When work was finished, we'd all rush to Marlborough Crescent to catch the bus back home to Winlaton. Every night, as soon as we walked through the back door, my Mother had a whopping dinner ready for us, and my how we'd demolish it. Then there would be a transformation: earrings, a pleated dress and our wedge heel sandals. We'd do our hair in the latest style and be ready to go back to Newcastle to go dancing at the Oxford Ballroom. My Mother would buy me a three-month bus pass so that I could use the buses at any time.

I remember going to the Oxford one night; there

was Rhoda, Pearl, Lily Morten and me and when we got off the bus at Newcastle these five Air Force lads got on talking to us, we called them the Brylcreem Boys as their hair was shining with Brylcreem. The lads came down to the Oxford with us.

The Oxford Ballroom, properly called the Oxford Galleries, was a great dance hall. Once you were inside you never got to sit on your bottom. "In the Mood" would start and then there was the Jitterbug. The sirens would go but no one paid them any attention. You just kept on dancing.

Then out at eleven o'clock for the last train from Newcastle Central Station along to Blaydon and the walk back up Blaydon Bank to home.

We'd walk down Clayton Street and it would be alive with soldiers and airmen. As they passed you, the Yanks would say: "Goodnight ma'am." But even though the streets would be teeming with soldiers far from their home, the atmosphere was friendly and you felt safe.

The train back to Blaydon left Newcastle Central Station at midnight and the station would be crammed with troops waiting for the troop-trains to take them off to their destinations. The trains ran all night. There would be young girls kissing their sweethearts and families waving their husbands, sons and brothers goodbye.

The same night we met the airmen, we got to talking to some soldiers while we were waiting for our train home. The soldiers were waiting for their train down to London. Roaming around the Central Station were the gigantic American Military Police too. The MPs were a lot taller than our lads, especially the coloured soldiers who were all about six foot four; they played a great part in the War. Apart from them being so tall, the MPs also wore a red band on their arm with MP on it in white. It was their job to look for soldiers who had overstayed their leave, arrest them and get them back to their battalion.

After we'd got off the train at Blaydon, we'd walk up Blaydon Bank and get back home at about half-past midnight. We'd have our supper and go straight to bed. Next morning Mum would shout us up at 6 o'clock and we'd go downstairs to the kitchen where she had our breakfast ready.

When we were sitting eating our breakfast she'd ask, 'Did you enjoy your dance?' and I'd tell her about what had happened the night before and we'd have a few laughs. One thing about my Mother, if you told her where you were going and what time you'd be home, then that was all right with her, she never spoiled our teenage lives.

We pretty much relaxed on a Sunday and had a long lie-in, not getting up until eight o'clock in the morning. I'd come downstairs with my curling pins in and would ask my Mother if she needed any help with the house but she'd always say: 'No, the dinner is cooking and everything else is done and dusted.'

Sunday daytime was always a lazy day but on Sunday night we would go to Ryton Willows, which was a small cafe down by the River Tyne. You could buy tea, coffee, ice cream and cakes there. It was a favourite haunt of young people and they'd come from all over: Ryton, Greenside and Blaydon as well as Winlaton.

Sometimes we'd go to the sixpenny hop at the YMCA Hut where I'd learned to tap-dance when I was younger. For the sixpenny hop, you'd pay your entrance and then you could dance. My sister Barbara would go with her friends and I would go with my friends and a few of the local lads. It was a night out.

One night a week, usually a Tuesday, I'd stay in and my Mum and I would have a good night. I'd wash my hair and have an early night. Sometimes I would pop down to see my Aunt Emily; she was married to my Mother's oldest brother, George Gilfillan, who was a miner. George and Emily had two sons, Alex and Arthur, who also worked in the coal mines. The miners were classed as essential workers and so they didn't get their call-up papers although they could volunteer to join-up if they wanted to.

My youngest brother Norman was a rugby player for Ryton Rugby club. His best friend was Bernard Sinclair but he got the nickname Ginger as his hair was really red and he had fair skin. Norman and Ginger were both big hefty fifteen stone lads as was another friend of theirs, Willy Simpson. When they'd finished their rugby, my brother would bring the two of them home for their tea and golly, they were good eaters! Ginger and Willy were miners and my brother who was fifteen years old was serving his time to be an engineer at Smith Patterson's.

I must tell you this. Before my brother became an engineer, he and a friend of his called Tom Robson got this job moving manure at this factory in Swalwell. Swalwell was about three and half miles away from Winlaton so they had to get the bus home.

Well when they got on the bus, the other people on the bus complained about the smell. This went on for a few weeks and mind you, my brother did smell. At the finish, they were not allowed on the bus and they had to walk the three and half miles home every night. They soon gave up these jobs and that's how my Dad got Norman his job at Smith Patterson's.

So we were all settled in our jobs and they were all good jobs; our pay was good and we gave it all to our Mother and we were all happy.

Norman's friend, Ginger, was always wanting to take me home from dances and he would ask my sister Barbara to ask me for him.

He would say to her: 'Ask Mary if I can take her home.'

I went out with him once or twice and after that he would come to my Mother's and say to my Mum: 'Mrs Hymers, will you get your Mary to come out with me?'

Or on the one night a week I stayed in, Ginger would knock on my Mum's door and she would open it and shout up the stairs:

'Mary there's someone to see you. Are you asleep?' and I'd shout down, 'Yes I am and I don't want to see him!'

open it and shout up the stairs:

'Mary there's someone to see you. Are you asleep?' and I'd shout down, 'Yes I am and I don't want to see him!'

Chapter 11
The War's Still On

I shall get back to my story. I was about sixteen and half and the War was still raging on across Europe where they were fighting hard. Of course, our side was winning. Of course it was.

But really, in Winlaton, we didn't know the half of what was going on with the war. We had air raids but nothing like the ones we'd seen on Pathé News. The Blitz in London, Coventry flattened, the cathedral gone, we saw that too. We read the newspapers and we'd find out bits from the soldiers who called in at our homes. We'd turn on the radio and there would be Lord Haw Haw, William Joyce, with his 'Germany calling, Germany calling,' and we'd listen to all the German propaganda over the radio and we'd be laughing at him saying: 'Here he is again!'

The reality was that despite all of this information we didn't really have a clue. My Mother would say:

'If they get here, I have a pill for each of us.'

But they never got this far and they could not handle the Russian winters either. That's what beat them in the end.

The soldiers who were stationed at Winlaton would go on manoeuvres, but as soon as they'd done their training, they were shipped abroad to do their duty in the War.

My brother Alex was in the Far East in Burma. My Mum had received a letter from him and when she read it, she shed a few tears; saying: 'Thank God he is alright,' and then she started to write him a letter back.

In one of her replies to him, my sister Barbara and I thought we'd drop him a line as well, not to ask how he was, but to see if he could get us each a pair of Eastern sandals. We sent Alex the measurements of our feet and though it was quite a few months before we got them; they did arrive. They were chocolate brown and we did write back and thank him.

Alex sent photographs; he was black with the sun. He never complained being there or said anything about wanting to come home; they all knew they had to stick it out. It was a long war. We never saw our brother for years. But we wrote him letters. He said Burma was a lovely country with much to see. There were lots of landmines. Lots of his friends blown up. He said it was horrendous. He said that some Air Force boys would be in lorries and the next time you looked, they'd been blown up by a mine.

As I've said, my brother Norman was a rugby player; all fifteen stone of him. He came home with black eyes, bruised knees. He once came home with a broken rib.

I asked him:

'How did this happen? Did they dance on top of you?'

He was taken to hospital and they strapped him up and he was off work for a few weeks.

Norman was always immaculately dressed. He had a Harris Tweed suit, it was sort of ginger colour, and he would wear it with brown brogue shoes, a beige shirt and a chocolate brown tie and waistcoat to match. All the men dressed smartly. My Grandfather and Father would dress in their best when they went for a drink on Saturday night. Everyone wore their suits and ties and always had polished shoes and Brylcreemed hair. The forties, my generation, were always well groomed.

We had better manners as well. Men would stand and give you their seats on a bus. We would never dream of not giving up our seat to an elderly person; we were taught to do that and to have respect for our elders. We never answered back to our parents or anyone older than us and we listened to what was said to us.

My sister Barbara was working in Armstrong's Munitions factory and she smoked cigarettes. She would hide them from my Mother in the outside toilet. There was a ledge above the door and Barbara would hide them on the ledge. Barbara would come in from work and my Mother would say: 'I can smell smoking. Have you been smoking?'

My sister would lie and say 'No,' but of course, my Mother knew she was lying and she'd get quite a rollicking about it.

It was something my Mother couldn't stand: women smoking and drinking. We never drank alcohol or went into a public house: ladies didn't then. But if we were going to bed then Barbara would open the front bedroom window and blow the smoke outside.

I would tease her and say, 'I'll tell Ma on you!' and she'd reply, 'If you do, I'll thump you!' but I never told my Mum about our Barbara smoking in the bedroom, because when I began my new job at Sinclair's, I smoked as well and if I'd told on Barbara she'd have told on me.

Everybody smoked then. We had our cigarette holders and we'd put our Craven A's or Players in them, and with our flimsy dresses and ankle-strap shoes, our lipstick and face powder we were like the film stars we watched: Betty Grable and Rita Hayworth.

We were good looking lasses, all of us, all slim because we all worked and walked and danced; it kept you fit. We never laid in bed, we were up at six o'clock in the morning, worked all day and then went dancing until midnight before going to bed and getting up with the larks again at six o'clock the next morning.

Barbara had a new boyfriend. He was called Alex Hunter but everyone called him Jock because he came from Maddison near Falkirk in Scotland. He was in the Eighth Army and had been sent to some far-flung places. His letters used to arrive via Airmail. He was away for four years and my sister wrote to him religiously.

I would say to our Barbara:

'If you love Alex, why go out with other boys? You cannot love him, not really. Not if you have crushes on other soldiers,' but Barbara would just shrug her shoulders and she still went out with other soldiers and had crushes on other boys.

I'd sometimes ask her, 'Can I come out with you?' but she'd always reply, 'No, you cannot. You are not coming out with me.'

Sometimes she'd go out with our cousin Peggy Higgins, Peggy was seeing a boy called Ted Burgess. He looked very young, about nineteen. It didn't last long.

I remember Barbara once went to the Oxford Dance and fell madly in love with this Coldstream Guard called Bob Bradley. She was in love with him, I was sure of it.

She said, 'I like Bob.'

I said, 'How can you be in love with Bob Bradley?'

Bob wanted to marry her, and at the time I think she would have married him, she was so struck on him. But she was young; she was only two years older than me. He did come to my Mother's and asked her if was it all right if they got married.

My Mother said: 'She's only eighteen but if you feel the same way after the war, you can please yourselves.'

In the end, Bob was sent abroad and so that died a sudden death and we were back to square one. But she was still writing to Reg Funnel in the Royal Fusiliers, Ted Ward and Jock Hunter as well. One thing about my sister, the boys all stuck to her. But later on as the months rolled by, she got fed up writing to all of them and so my Mother wrote the letters for her instead.

We had found the address of a soldier called Jimmy who wanted a penfriend. So I wrote to him, and much to my surprise, I got a letter back from him. He asked if I would send him a photograph. I sent Jimmy a Jerome's photograph and wrote to him for two years; when I think back, my photographs must be around the world!

Even though we'd never met, he was very kind although in his head I think he thought I was his girlfriend. As far as I was concerned though, he was just a friend and if Mary said he was a friend then he was a friend.

Jimmy sent me numerous presents from the Middle East, a lovely handbag, and I think that I must have been one of the first girls in England to have an umbrella that folded up. He sent lots of jewellery too: Hawaiian beads in emerald green and white, blue and white, and red and white which were lovely to wear for my dances.

My sister's boyfriends were serving in the Middle East. Jimmy Pratt, my penfriend, was abroad. London was getting blitzed with doodlebugs but it did not stop our fun.

On a Saturday afternoon we'd all trot off to the Oxford which was a beautiful dance hall, or we'd go to the Melvane, which was another dance hall. Or we would go to the Empire Theatre in Newcastle where you could watch your favourite star in a good variety show. We were never bored with life. There were a lot of cinemas too: the Westgate, the Odeon, the Pavilion and the Essoldo. There were ice-cream parlours where you could have coffee, cakes and ices.

But we always ended at the Oxford Dance Hall. The favourite dance was the Conga. You'd begin it and by the end you were all in one great line shouting: 'Aye, Aye, Conga!' There was every nationality in that Conga: Yanks, Aussies, Canadians, Polish Airmen. We did the Rhumba and the Foxtrot as well, so you never got to sit down. The dance would finish at about 5pm on a Saturday afternoon and then when we came out the question was always, 'Where do we go next?' It was a great laugh.

One Saturday, my cousin, Peggy Higgins, and I came out of the Oxford and got talking to two RAF officers. One was blonde and one had black hair and they were called Ron and Bill. They'd only have been about twenty-three or twenty-four and they were pilots and nice lads, very well spoken. They asked us where we were going and we told them that we hadn't decided yet but we were going for a coffee and sandwich and then we were thinking of either going to see a film or we'd go to the Melvane Dance Hall. They asked if they could join us, and of course we said yes.

So we went to have our coffee and sandwich at Mark Toney's in Newcastle, and while we were there Peggy and I went to the ladies to wash our faces, put a bit more muck on and have a bit of a giggle together and then off we all went to another dance and had a great time.

We walked down to Central Station to catch the last train back to Blaydon station and said our goodbyes and exchanged addresses.

Bill and Ron were off to London on the Sunday to join their squadron and we promised to write to them and them to us. Their train to London came in before ours did so we waved them off and then we got our own train and came home. I was starved as two sandwiches in Mark Toney's hadn't filled me up, not after all the dancing, but my good old Mum had a lovely cup of tea and boiled ham and salad waiting for me.

She said: 'I thought you'd have come home after the afternoon dance but as long as you've enjoyed yourself.'

Occasionally we'd cross the fields and go down into Newburn. There was a picture house there and we'd go to the pictures with our young men but they were only friends. Alex Dawson, Johnny Weddle, they worked on the railway at Blaydon. If they passed us when they were on the engine, they'd shout at us and wave.

I had a crush on Johnny Weddle and Alex Dawson had a crush on me, but it never came to anything. He would always dance with me, but at home time, I'd disappear. I would never go out with anyone, they never appealed to me. All of our boyfriends were decent. A goodnight kiss was the limit and the young men would respect that. I think my generation were the best. In my day we had dignity and I think we had more fun. We never heard of rape or young girls having babies at fifteen years of age, I think that our Mothers and Fathers had a better way of organising our lives.

I think that sometimes the Geordies had no manners. At a dance they'd come up to you and say things like, 'Hoy, ye getting' up?' and I'd shake my head and slink away.

In fact, thinking back on it now, really and truthfully speaking, I never in my life courted an Englishman. Some of the soldiers were different, more polite but as I was only sixteen years old, I never really thought of dating anyone. Seriously, you are free at that age.

Chapter 12
No More Jeeps

We'd go anywhere for a good dance. At Sunniside near Whickham there was a dance held at the Catholic Church Hall on a Sunday night. Of course, it meant that we had to go to church first before we were allowed into the dance. The Catholic Father would say:

'Come to Church first and then you can come to our dance.'

So we'd go to the Catholic Church, despite the fact that it wasn't our parish, and none of us were Catholics. But there was nothing wrong in going to church. I've always loved going Church. I went to St Paul's Protestant Church in Winlaton every Sunday and I've never had any bother saying my prayers morning, noon and night.

The Catholics put on a good dance at Sunniside. There was a piano, accordion, drums. Doreen

Steadman usually went with me. Doreen was very good at dancing. There were plenty of young men to ask you to dance with them but the main dance we did was the Bradford Barn: two steps in, two steps out, turn around and on to the next partner. By the time you'd completed the dance you knew everyone. As it was a Sunday, the dance finished early. Ten o'clock on a Sunday night. If we wanted to stay to the end of the dance then we'd miss the last bus to Winlaton so we'd catch the bus down the bank to Swalwell and then walk from Swalwell along to Winlaton Mill and up the bank to Winlaton.

Sometimes we would go down by old Winlaton Mill in the day. We walk across the stepping-stones and have a paddle to wet our feet. I'd go there with Doreen Steadman too. Doreen was a good friend; I could rely on her. She worked at Sinclair's with me. She never bothered boys. She was very shy, very decent and we sort of stuck together. She was a long time friend.

Doreen and I would go around with some girls from Blaydon Burn, Lily, Rhoda and Marion. We would just hop on a bus into Newcastle and decide what to do once we got there. One time Lily suggested that we went to the all-in wrestling.

Rhoda asked, 'How much is it to get in?'

Lily didn't know.

Marion said, 'Does there many go?'

Lily said she didn't know.

I asked Lily, 'Is it rough?'

Lily said she had no idea, as she'd never been before.

So we didn't have a clue what to expect, but we went to the wrestling anyway.

We went into the cheap end, the balcony. It was a huge place, packed solid with a square ring in the middle. Some people had front seats. The referee came into the middle of the ring and said who the wrestlers were and then in they came and it began. Rhoda, Lillian, Marion and I began to giggle. There was jeering and booing, then the audience began to throw cans at them. Some were saying it was a put-up job. Oh enough. This didn't appeal to me. Not Mary's cup of tea. The other girls didn't like it either so we came out during the interval.

But where to go next? It was too late for a film or a dance, but too early to go home. How about Mark Toney's? So Mark Toney's and ice cream it was. We met some Aussie Air Force guys who were stationed at Whitley Bay along the coast. We enjoyed their company and had a walk around Newcastle until it was nearly time for our midnight train. We said our farewells at Newcastle Central Station. It was packed, as usual with soldiers and navy. Our train came in and we arranged to meet our Aussies at the Odeon on Sunday night as the Squadronaires Air Force Dance Band were playing and they were a good band.

When I got back, my Mum was waiting at the front door. She knew all the girls, so we were all chatting away together, the girls telling her about the wrestling and the Aussies we'd met. As we were standing chatting, two other ladies joined us: Nancy Merry and Edna Fraser. Nancy and Edna were older than my sister Barbara and they were having a great time telling my Mother about their night. My cousin, George Gilfillan, was with them. George was the same age as my eldest brother Alex. He was a superb dancer and singer.

He said to my Mother, 'Sina, I've met this gorgeous girl, she's absolutely beautiful.'

My Mother replied, 'Have you George?' and Nancy and Edna laughed and then Edna said:

'Sina, that was my Mother. We'll call in tomorrow and tell you our news.'

By now, it was well past midnight. Good job it was a Saturday night and I could lie in bed until eight o'clock on Sunday morning.

Another Saturday night and another new dress. This one was green brocade with a Peter Pan collar and a pleated skirt. I was off to the Greenside Dance with some friends of mine, the Browns, who lived down Blaydon Burn. I walked down to the Burn and knocked at the door of the Browns.

The Browns were quite a large family and Lily was really the one who was my friend. When I knocked at the door of the Browns', Lily's sister older sister, Evelyn, answered the door. I had on my new dress, my big earrings and my suede shoes and I said to Evelyn:

'Are you ready for the dance?'

But Evelyn said, 'Go home and change your dress, then you can go to the dance with us.'

Well it was the on the tip of my tongue to say me-ow but instead I went home and when my Mum said, 'You're back quick,' I said:

'I've had a really good laugh,' and told her what Evelyn had said.

Then I said to my Mum, 'I'm going to the dance, it's just coming back along that lonely road.'

My Mum said, 'Go to the dance and your Dad and I will meet you coming back.'

So off I went to the dance and I had a great time, and on the way back my Mother and Father were there to meet me and walk me home. As we came down Sandy Banks the sirens went off, the search lights came out and it was lovely linking my Mother and Father walking back home.

When we got back home, we had our supper and my Mum said: 'I enjoyed the walk.' Happy Days. Lovely Memories.

As we were sitting down to our supper, my sister Barbara came in and she'd had a great time too. She always said she'd had a great time when she came back from a dance.

Barbara usually went with her friend Doris and often Doris would come back home with her and they were usually giggling. If there were any air raids on in the village, Barbara and Doris would disappear and go off out visiting their friends.

When they got back, my Mother would say to them:

'What have you been up to?' and they'd sit down and tell my Mother where they'd been.

That night they'd been out and met these soldiers who had taken an Army Jeep out. Doris was in the back with her soldier and my sister Barbara had been in the front with her soldier. They'd been going down Blaydon Bank, which was a very steep bank. The brakes of the Jeep hadn't worked, and so they'd had to jump out of the Jeep while it was still going. They'd scraped their knees but they were in hysterics laughing and the pair of them saying: 'No more Jeeps.'

Chapter 13
A Trip To London

Saturday night was a full house for my Mum. My Grandfather would call and my Uncle Joseph, my Mother's youngest brother, would probably pop in too. He was a free spirit was Joseph. He never went out with women but he liked a gamble and a drink. They all had supper at our house, and my Mother always had a good table. She would cook two rabbits with hock so that the gravy turned to gelatine. There would be salad too. My Father's lettuces were like cabbages, and there would be tomatoes, spring onions and cucumbers as well. My Granny Emma would also visit my Mum's, but on Saturday night my Gran would go home early.

Through the week, my old Gran would come from Blaydon Burn to buy her groceries in our village. Her favourite shop was Walter Wilson's where she'd buy her favourite cooked ham; they sold beautiful cooked ham and my Gran was partial to a slice or two. She'd buy a few groceries and she'd say to the manager of the shop, Thomas Metcalfe he was called but everyone called him Tommy, she'd say to him:

'Tommy, put them on the bill and I will pay you at the weekend.'

On her way back home my Gran would call in at my Mum's for a cup of tea and later my Mother would laugh and say to us: 'That cooked ham never reached Blaydon Burn, it was eaten at 2 Manor Terrace.'

Sometimes I'd walk my Gran back home. Through the Gun Huts and past the allotments we would go. She was very slow with her bad leg and she'd put her old hands on my shoulders so she could lean on me.

On my days off, I'd often trot down to my Gran's to keep her company. Sometimes we went to visit her relation over in Sunderland; her name was Etty Bagnall. Etty gave me two fantail doves for my brother, Norman. Etty had a daughter my age called Jean, who was a good friend of mine.

My brother Norman was pleased with his two fantails. My Father made a small hut in the coalhouse for them. Of course they were spoilt rotten but I think my Mum thought it was cruel to have them locked up so she must have given them to someone who kept pigeons and had a proper place for them on their allotment. Nearly all the men in the village had an allotment and grew their own vegetables and most of them kept pigeons.

Sometimes my Uncle Douglas, my Father's brother, would visit our house. Once he said: 'Sina, we'll have a high tea,' as he was staying for a few hours.

I asked my Mum what a high tea was and she told me: 'That's where they stand on the table and jump off.'

She had some queer sayings sometimes.

When all the men got together, they would all sit down and argue politics. My Father was a Conservative and my Grandfather Gilfillan was Labour so there were some lively conversations.

For me, it was Saturday night every night. I was thoroughly enjoying my teenage life. I'd meet my friend Doreen at a dance hall and everyone was dancing the Jitterbug. It was a Yankee dance and if you had a good Yank who really knew how to dance the Jitterbug you were quids in. They threw you on their hips, the left side, then the right and then they'd have both your arms and would throw you through their legs. They kept hold of you but with the dance floor being like glass you'd slither back through again. It was great fun and we were definitely never short of exercise. I always thought dancing was great. If you feel miserable, go to a dance. None of this Cowboy dancing, a proper dance where you can rhumba the night away and after that, the last dance: "Who's taking you home tonight?"

I met this young man Leslie. He was in the Air Force and quite good looking and he took me home from a dance. He was billeted in Winlaton and I had arranged to see him the night after the dance as he was being posted abroad the day after that. We did go to see a film and I sat beside him but I had sly looks at him during the film and I said to myself: 'Not your type Mary.'

When we said goodbye at the end of the night, Leslie said:

'I shall write to you.'

I said, 'Do not expect me to write. I am not good at writing.'

But he wrote to me and my Mum wrote back to him for me.

We had a happy home. Barbara, my sister, worked at Armstrong's Munitions factory, my brother Norman was serving his time to be an Engineer, my oldest brother Alex was in Burma and I had a good job at John Sinclair's cigarettes factory. I had a lot of friends at Sinclair's and I often went to dances with them after work.

There was a ballroom dance on at the old Assembly Rooms in Newcastle so the girls at Sinclair's all bought tickets for the dance. As usual, Newcastle was busy with troops coming in and moving out again. In fact, now I think of it, we met more people with this war than we ever met again in our lives.

The dance was on a Friday night and Friday was the day we got our weekly wage packet. Everyone got paid on a Friday. I never opened my pay packet and neither did my sister, we gave it straight to our Mother and she gave us our pocket money for the week. We paid for our own dance entrance or pictures with our pocket money, but our Mother bought our three monthly bus passes and our clothes as well, although we got to choose what we liked.

I got all toffed up for the dance and went back into the Town. It was a beautiful dance hall, the old Assembly Rooms, a massive stone-built building with lovely old-fashioned stairs and large columns around the hall. You could imagine ladies in years gone by in crinoline dresses coming down the big stairs and dancing in the Hall.

Well, we had a great time at the dance and during it, I was talking to a young girl from my work. Her name was Margaret Cross. I'd known her since I started at Sinclair's and she was very quiet was Margaret but this night she surprised me because she said:

'Mary, would you like to go to London for your holidays?'

It turned out that she had an aunt down in Essex that we could stay with. So, I said that I'd ask my Mother about it when I got back and let her know.

Of course, my Mother said yes, and so Margaret and I took our two weeks holiday from Sinclair's together, packed a few clothes and went to London. We each had about twenty pounds spending money although our train fares came out of that, and my Mother had told me before I went that I was to write if I needed any more money.

We got the train from Newcastle Central Station to London Kings Cross and then we managed to get the tube to Grays in Essex. Very busy was London, troops everywhere and you could see that it had been well bombed. There were a lot of women in uniform, khaki, navy and midnight blue, and if we saw a sailor, we would touch his collar for luck. Margaret's cousins met us at the station. They were older than we were but very kind as was Margaret's auntie.

The cousins took us to visit Gravesend. We took a ferry across, and it was a quaint place, cobblestones and all the shops were like curiosity shops. Margaret and I took the Tube into London as well and saw all of the sights: Big Ben, the Houses of Parliament and Buckingham Palace and the Mall.

We were stood on the Mall when two Yanks came up and introduced themselves saying that they were on leave and looking around London and asked if we would join them for a cup of tea and we said we would.

We all went into a cafe and we were starving. The Yanks said that they were going to have steak and chips and asked if we wanted something to eat too, and we said yes, as I was so hungry I could have eaten a horse. We were about half-way through our meal when the young chap I was with; he was called Skippy, said: 'I hope you're good at washing dishes.'

I looked at Margaret aghast because I was thinking: 'Oh my God!' as it was nearing the end of our stay and we were running short of money by this time.

Then Skippy roared with laughter and said: 'Gee Mary if you could only see your face!' and we all roared with laughter too, but Margaret and I must have looked a picture for a moment or two.

When we'd finished our tea we went to the Covent Garden Dance Hall and it was a lovely ballroom. We had a few dances and then, as it was about six o'clock at night and summer, we thought we'd like to see Hyde Park so we all went there before the Yanks walked us to the Tube station.

I think that the two boys had overstayed their leave as whenever we saw an MP we had to dodge them and there were a lot of MPs in London. We exchanged addresses; Skippy came from Massachusetts, although I didn't think I'd ever hear from him again.

The next day we went back into London to go to the Palladium to see Vic Oliver. The theatre was packed solid and we thoroughly enjoyed the show, the dancing and the costumes.

Towards the end of our holiday I wanted to buy my Mother a present, so I found a wooden tray with a glass top that had a picture of an old-fashioned lady in a crinoline dress on it. She was in a garden with Canterbury bells and there were blue and silver roses on the glass top of the tray; it was really pretty. For my Father I bought cigarettes as at the time he smoked. But by now we were really broke and although we'd enjoyed our holiday, I was looking forward to coming home.

We travelled back home on a Saturday, first to Kings Cross and then by train to Newcastle arriving home safe and sound.

When she saw me my Mother said, 'I expected you to write for more money,' but although I was broke by the end of the trip I would never have done that. I knew they'd scraped together the twenty pounds they gave me; it was a fortune then.

So I told her that I'd managed and that I'd had a lovely time and had seen everything I wanted to see and then I gave her the tray and my Dad the cigarettes.

I told my Mother and Father about meeting the two Yanks and what had happened at the meal, and I told them about dodging the MPs as well. Then I said to my Mother:

'If any letters come from Skippy then that's who it is and you know all about him now.'

I settled in at home and on Monday I was back at work where I saw Margaret, who asked if I'd had a good time with her. I said that I'd had a lovely time because I had, and told her again how kind her aunt had been to us, because she wouldn't take any board from us for our keep for the whole time we were there.

So now I was writing to Leslie in the Air Force, Jimmy in the Middle East and now the Yank, Skippy but none of them were serious for me. I was pretty hard to please. If I did not like who I went out with, I didn't go out with them again.

My sister was different to me. She had umpteen boyfriends and quite a few of them wanted to marry her. But at sixteen years of age, men didn't interest me. I would not be impolite, but if they arranged to see me, I would go out with them a few times, look them over and usually find something wrong with them; they weren't my style or their feet were too big and so it would be goodbye.

We never got bored. We would rise early, bed late; there was always plenty of activity going on. You never heard of anyone being burgled; you could leave your door unlocked. We were not rich. But no one was. The housewife was the captain of the household, the cook, the organizer, and the bill payer. The husband was the breadwinner. As teenagers, our life was work in the day, every night fun.

But then on the news you heard of young soldiers being shot, killed, taken prisoner. My cousin Peggy Higgins married Jack Tulloch. He was captured at Dunkirk and spent four years in the Prisoner Of War camps. They were made to walk a few hundred miles, about five hundred I think.

I said to him once, 'Jack, all those miles,' and he laughed and said:

'Aye, it was a canny hike, but there were a lot of us and I enjoyed it. I saw countries I've never seen although a lot of it was well flattened.'

Jack was a happy young man; it took a lot to discourage him.

Chapter 14
Sinclairs Tobacco Factory

As well as Margaret, I had a lot of friends at Sinclair's. There were a few thousand girls worked for John Sinclair; he was a good boss and for the time it was good money. I would knock around with the girls I worked with, Audrey Hemmings, Doreen Rutherford, Bettie Story, Evelyn Dennis, and Ethel Gibson. Ethel died very young as she contracted TB poor soul; she had a lovely voice. We would say to her, 'Sing Ethel,' and she'd be off singing. We'd all go out together in Newcastle to dances and films.

When our lunch break came, we'd sometimes go to a cafe. We only had an hour so it was a bit of a rush if we did this but we'd go to Lockhart's Cafe and buy pie and chips and a cup of tea and a sweet like apple pie and custard

I got moved about a lot in Sinclair's. I was on the hoists for a few months; this was where all of the great barrels of dried tobacco were hoisted in from outside. There was an opening in the wall and a lorry would pull up outside loaded with crates of tobacco. The men who worked at Sinclair's would fill the hoist with tobacco and when it was full, I'd take it to the top floor where the barrels would be opened and the tobacco would be spread out to soften.

Tobacco is like dried hard wood and when it came into Sinclair's it was emptied out of the barrels and spread on a large stone floor where after a few days it would soften up. Tobacco leaves are quite large and have a thick stalk down the middle of them. The girls in my department would remove the stalk and once that was done it would depart from our floor into the next department.

After a while, they moved me from working the hoists to be with Betty Spoor in Billy Hall's department. This was where the unsold cigarettes were returned. Our job was to take the paper off the cigarettes, open them out and then tease out the tobacco into a pile of shag. Billy would put the shag tobacco on a wire mesh on top of a long tray and the tray was taken to a warm room that was separate from our department. It was left there for a few days before being turned into snuff. After that, I was in the spinning room where Rubicon Twist was made; I could go on and on but so much for my job. When you got home, everything was forgotten. Your job was gone and your life was about enjoying yourself.

The owner of Sinclair's factory where I worked, John Sinclair, was good to his girls and twice a year we got a good bonus. He used to say: 'I'd rather share my profit with my workers than given it the Government.'

I remember that with one of my bonuses I got after the War finished, I bought a costume in the 'New Look' style which was considered very daring after all the years of the War. This new fashion was to have a dress with long sleeves that were very tight fitting on your arms and a skirt that reached your ankles with many yards of material in the skirt to make it look fully flared. My coat was also flared from the waist down. Four inches from the hemline were black satin ribbons that had been embroidered on the skirt and my coat sleeves also had four satin ribbons on it.

Everyone dressed in the latest fashion and it was a bit of a competition amongst us to see who had the best dress. There were some very smart young ladies too and we were all slim although we never dieted. All our dancing kept us slim and we walked a lot and of course the majority of us were up very early, six o'clock in the morning to be exact, and at work full-time all day and dancing all night. We were pretty fit, and even at ninety, I am still pretty slim.

I'd received a letter from Skippy the Yank I met in London. I was surprised. I hadn't expected to hear from him. With Skippy, I had three penfriends, him, Leslie the Airman and Jimmy Pratt. They all wrote to me all through the war and they all had my photographs. Skippy sent me his picture. My

Mother thought he was good looking.

He wrote: 'Mary, after the War, I want you to come to the States and marry me.' He said he loved me!

I said, 'You're nuts, you don't know me,' but I never wrote this in my letters, I only thought it.

My penfriend from Sunderland, Jimmy Pratt, wrote to tell me that he had told his Mother about me too. Why Jimmy had told his Mother about me I do not know. There was nothing in my head about romance. They were penfriends. Soldiers in the middle of the war. I only wrote to them to be friendly. I was too young to be going out with anyone seriously, in fact I was more your happy-go-lucky type than a romantic sort.

But we were moving on to victory in the War. We had seen news that the Germans invaded Poland, Ukraine, Latvia but we never knew the half of what was going on over on the Continent. We were lucky in our lives. We were free in England and I will shout about this from the rooftops. We could go anywhere we wanted, work, dancing, films, shopping. Yes, there was the blackout and air raid shelters and rationing but we all managed. Everyone helped each other.

Chapter 15
The End of the War

I reached seventeen and everyone was celebrating peace in the world. There were parties all over; everyone went crazy. All the soldiers would be coming home; they'd been away for years. They stopped the War in the Jap Territory too, by dropping an atom bomb on Hiroshima. There were thousands dead, but my brother and all the forces who'd been stationed across in Jap Country were coming home. All those who'd been captured and put in the Japanese concentration camps were like walking skeletons. The Japs were a cruel people.

That same year my old Granny Gilfillan had taken ill. My Gran had a very bad stroke and it had left her paralysed. She always looked ill. She had an ulcerated leg all her life too, God love her, and her life had been very hard. My Mum had been looking after her while she was ill but then my Granny died. That left my Grandfather and Uncle Joseph to be looked after, and so they came to lunch at my Mother's every day. My Mum had their shopping and washing and cleaning to do as well as her own.

When my oldest brother Alex returned from the War, my Mother had got him a small prefab to live in. It had two bedrooms, a sitting room and back kitchen. He'd married his WAAF Jean Cummings and they had a little girl Sandra, her full name was Alexandria. Our Sandra was a beautiful little girl. I would go around on a Sunday morning and take my little niece out in her pram. My Mother spoilt her and when our Barbara got married, my Mum would take Sandra off on holiday to Scotland. Mum was in her element when she had our Sandra staying.

Alex had only been back in England for a few days when my Gran died and he'd come up from London to go to her funeral. He loved his old Gran did our Alex but he had to go back to London after the funeral to get his official demob papers.

All the men coming home meant that they all had to look for jobs. But there was lots of work. There were plenty factories: engineering, plumbing, steel industries, and then there were the coal mines too. My brother Alex went back into the coal mines when he got back and I know he hated it, that's why he had joined the Air Force. But with a wife and child to support, he had no choice and so back to the mines he went, I think with a heavy heart.

Later he improved his position and became a lot higher than a coal miner but it took a lot of study at night school after a hard day's work. Eventually he became Manager of a few coal mines, and when he moved around managing the mines there was always a beautiful house to go with the job.

Even though the War had finished, young boys were still getting their call-up papers and most of them had two years conscription to do across in Germany or Japan. You had a choice. You could do two years as a conscript or two years as a Bevan boy down in the mines.

In the meantime, there was my sister's boyfriend to think about. Jock Hunter was on his way home so my sister had to stop her shenanigans of going out with different boys.

One Saturday I had been to a dance at Blaydon Miners Hall and Ginger Duffy had brought me home.

It was eleven o'clock at night and we were outside.

'Goodnight Ginger,' I said.

But Ginger said:

'My name is Bernie and I'm not letting you go in unless you see me tomorrow night.'

So I said, 'If you don't let me go in I will shout for my Mother and she'll crack you one.'

Then the back door opened and my Mother shouted for me. This was at eleven thirty. So I shouted back to her:

'He won't let me come in Mum'.

'Let her come in Bernie,' my Mother told him, to

which he replied:

'Mrs Hymers, can she see me tomorrow night?'

Of course my Mother was laughing and saying 'Yes' but I said:

'I am not. I don't like you.'

My Mother was still laughing when I came into the house and she said:

'Well, that was straight, but you shouldn't have hurt the lads feelings like that.'

But what could I do? I didn't like him and I didn't want to go out with him and if Mary doesn't like a boy then they won't see her again.

We had supper and I went to bed and a bit later on my sister Barbara came up to bed. Now that everyone was home, we slept two to a bed again. We were all snuggled in for the night but we were awakened at about two-thirty in the morning by a rat-tat on the door. The house was raised. My sister Barbara turned to me in bed and said: 'I bet I know who that is.'

Me being dumb, said, 'Who?' and Barbara said, 'I bet that's Alex Hunter,' and then she went 'Ugh...'

'What did you say that for?' I asked.

'I'll have to be getting married,' she told me.

'Do you love him?' I asked her, and Barbara said 'No.'

'You're nuts,' I told her. ' I know I'm nuts but you're worse nuts than me. You've put the wedding banns in at Church and you don't love him. So why are you marrying him?'

Our Barbara said, 'Well I said I would so now I'll have to go through with it.'

That seemed daft to me, so I said to Barbara:

'I'm going to tell our Mother that you don't love him and she'll put a stop to it.'

But Barbara said, 'If you tell my Mother that I don't love him and I don't want to marry him then I'll thump you.'

Well I never told my Mother, and Barbara got married at St Paul's Church in Winlaton. She married Alex by special licence as you could do that during and just after the War and then she went back to his house in Polmont in Scotland. At first, they lived in two rooms that were let to them by Mrs Hunter but after a few months, they got a prefab in Polmont.

With our Barbara married and our Alex off with his wife there were only two of us at home with my Mum and dad: my baby brother Norman and me. It was quiet. I had the bed all to myself in the front bedroom and Norman had his bed all to himself in the back bedroom. But apart from that life went on as normal and we all went about our business.

Barbara and Alex weren't the only ones getting married now the War was over. Some of the girls I'd known had married their soldier sweethearts and gone off to live down in London. A lot of the girls I knew married Yanks and went off to the States. I was too young to die. I was still hearing from Jimmy Pratt, Leslie the Airman and Skippy the Yank who I'd met down in London, but I still wasn't in love with any of them.

Chapter 16
Achim

Opposite my Mother's house was a farm and this farm belonged to Mrs Snarr. When I was younger old Mrs Stoke had lived there with her two sons, Tommy and John, and her daughter Violet, but they had moved when the War started and the farm now belonged to Mrs Snarr and her sons, Eddie and John.

It was a Saturday morning, the War had been over for about six months, and I was just about to go to Newcastle for the day. I was standing beside the front door in the little bit of garden at the front of the house and I was just getting ready to set off, when my Mum said to me:

'Mary, there's a young man standing staring at you. He's standing in Mrs Snarr's garden where the wooden huts are.'

I asked her, 'Mum how can you see him?' because

she was in the house and my Mum said:

'I'm looking out the front window and he's not taken his eyes off you. I think it's a young German lad.'

So, I looked across over the fields into Mrs Snarr's garden and there he was, and he waved at me.

It was a German lad, a prisoner of war. We knew this because they had to wear different coloured patches on their backs so that we could tell who they were.

I thought, 'I'm not waving to him, he's a German,' and I just stood there. My Mum had come outside to join me by now and she gave me a nudge with her elbow.

'Are you not waving back?' she asked.

'No,' I said. 'He's a German and the enemy so I'm not waving to him.'

'Now honey,' she said to me. 'He's someone's bairn and he has a Mother and a Father just like you do. And his Mother will be worrying about him just like I worried about our Alex. So you can wave back.'

Well after my Mother said that, I didn't have much choice so I sort of half-waved back to him and waited to see what he would do next.

Now across the road from where I was standing was this crickety old wall, and he came down and I could see that he had this small note in his hand. There were a few stones missing from this wall and the German slipped this note in a small space where there was a stone missing and then he headed back up the field. Well it was one thing to wave at him but once there was a note, of course I wanted to see what was in it so I crossed the road. But I wasn't going to let him see that I was desperate to read his note, so I picked it up out of the hole in the wall and then I walked back to our house, but I knew that he was watching me as I crossed the road back to our house.

When I opened up the note it read: 'Come to the bottom of the field so that I can talk to you'

'Well?' said my Mum, 'What does the note say?'

I passed it across to her and she read it and then said, 'Well go on then, go and talk to the lad.'

I looked across at him from my Mum's front door and he pointed for me to go and meet him at the end of the field. So I walked back across the road and down to the end of the field, and he was there waiting for me.

'Hello Mary,' he said.

I was a bit surprised at this and said, 'You know my name?'

'Mrs Snarr said your name was Mary.' he told me, then he said, 'I see you coming home from work when I wait for my bus to take us back to camp.'

His English was perfect. Blonde, about six foot four. He wore glasses, he was tanned, he was rather nice looking actually.

'Where is your camp?' I asked.

'High Spen,' he said. 'Will you meet me there tonight?'

'I wouldn't know where in High Spen your camp was,' I told him. Then I added, 'What is your name?'

He told me his name was Achim.

'Well Achim,' I said, 'I generally go to a dance on Saturday night but I shall change my arrangements and yes, I'll come to see you,' although I was thinking, 'this is a daft date I'm setting on.'

'Do not forget Mary,' said Achim.

'I won't forget.' I promised, and so we parted and I walked back across the road to our house.

My Mother was waiting for me; she'd watched me meet him out of the front room window.

'Well, what happened?' she asked.

I told her.

'He wants to see me tonight, but he's still the enemy,' I said.

Well I'm sure my Mother was as daft as me because she said:

'There's no enemy now honey, the War is over and you can please yourself.'

'In that case, I'll go,' I told her. 'It's a daft date but his English is superb, better than mine and he's rather nice, so I shall go on a daft date,' and at six o'clock that night I boarded the bus to High Spen.

High Spen was about four miles away from my

house and the bus took about twenty minutes to get there. When I got to High Spen there were five young ladies standing waiting at the bus stop, and as I got off the bus, they all said together: 'Are you Mary?'

Well I had to be, didn't I, there was no one else on the bus. But I said, 'Yes, I am.'

They told me that Achim had sent them to meet me off the bus. I smiled at them and then said:

'You must all have boyfriends at the camp then?'

They all laughed back at me. '

Yes we do,' they told me.

'But do you take them seriously?' I asked them.

'Well,' said one of the girls who I later found out was called Mary. 'I've been going out with Richard for about three months now and Joyce has been seeing Helmut for about the same time.'

'Where do we meet them?' I asked, and Mary and the other girls said, 'Follow us.'

We walked down from the bus stop to an embankment where there was a stile and then followed a brook that ran through a woodland into a field full of tents and there was Achim and his friends.

Achim introduced me to his friends. They clicked their heels and then shook my hand.

'Crikey!' I thought, 'well this is a first.'

'We will go higher up into the fields so our Sergeant

and Corporal cannot see us.' Achim said.

We did and when we'd walked to the top of the field, away from the tents, we all sat down and chatted. Their English was very good.

'What is your surname Mary?' asked Achim.

'My name is Mary Hymers,' I told him.

'That is peculiar,' said Achim. 'My name is Heimar too. Hans Achim Heimer.'

'We could be cousins,' I said.

Achim laughed and said:

'I don't think so. But it is a coincidence.'

We sat and talked for a while and then I said, 'I have to go for my bus at ten-thirty.'

Really I didn't need to get home so early, normally I'd get the midnight train back from Newcastle but the buses from High Spen stopped early and also I didn't want to look too eager. Achim walked me back to the High Spen bus stop.

When we got to the bus stop he said, 'Mary will you come to see me tomorrow? Sunday night? If you get off at the Barlow bus stop I shall walk along and meet you.'

'I don't want you to get into trouble' I told him, because I knew that they weren't supposed to go out of bounds, and Barlow, which was about a mile away from High Spen, would definitely be out of bounds to the prisoners.

'Sunday is always a quiet night,' said Achim.

'Sometimes they look around the camp but really the Sergeant and Corporal Geoff are pretty good.'

When I got home my Mother was waiting for me with my supper: a lovely ham that she had cooked and salad from my Father's allotment. I really enjoyed that. My Father wasn't home to have supper with us as my Grandfather had been for his supper and my Father had walked him home as my Grandfather was now over eighty.

While I had my supper, I told my Mother about my Saturday night outing.

'He was very polite. I'm meeting him tomorrow,' I told her. 'Works as an interpreter for the camp and does some of their office work as well. From Baden Baden. He's unusual. Different. I'm not taking it seriously.'

'Oh and his name is the same as mine' I added.

'How strange,' said my Mum.

'Hymers is a German name. He's not married either' I said.

My Mum was shocked.

'Our Mary you didn't ask him that did you?' she asked.

I said, 'Of course I did. If he was married or had a girlfriend I would not go out with him.'

Mary, Joyce and I continued seeing the prisoners. It was a laugh. Time passed and summer moved into September. The days were getting cooler but it was still a lovely month.

One Saturday night I met Achim with the other girls as usual and we decided to go into the woodland where it would be a bit warmer with the trees around. It was starting to get pretty dark so it must have been about nine o'clock when we heard footsteps.

Achim said, 'Shh! There's someone not very far away.'

We all kept pretty still and none of us said a word. Then, all of a sudden, these torches flashed on us. It was the Sergeant and Geoff the Corporal. We were flabbergasted!

'Ah-ha,' said the Sergeant.

'Ah-ha,' I said back at him, and we all laughed.

The Sergeant wasn't laughing.

'What's your name?' he asked.

'Mary Hymers,' I answered him.

'Well Mary,' said the Sergeant, 'you aren't supposed to be here. None of you'

'Why not?' I said.

'Because you're fraternizing with the enemy,' he told me.

I said, 'How can we be fraternizing? There's not a War on anymore.'

He wasn't amused.

'I shall have to write to tell your Mother where you've been,' he said to me.

'You do that,' I told him.

He went round and asked everyone their names and wrote them down along with our addresses. Then he made Achim and all the rest of the prisoners go back to the camp but to me and the girls he said, 'Come and have a cup of tea in the Sergeant's hut.'

Well we didn't want to be rude, so Joyce, Mary and I all trooped along to the hut and had a cup of tea with the Sergeant and the Corporal.

We were just on our way out when the Corporal, Geoff, beckoned to me.

'Mary would you come out with me one night?' he asked.

'No!' I said to him.

Well that finished our party in the woods and we all went back to my friend Mary's house and laughed about what had happened, because really, when the torches shone in our faces we did get a heck of a shock.

'The Sergeant took your name and said he'd write to your Mother,' said Mary. 'Will you get into trouble?'

'No,' I said. 'My Mum knows where I go and who I go with and she trusts me anyway. Will they get into trouble?'

Ethel laughed, 'Well if they do, I doubt it will stop them. There's half the camp get the bus to Newcastle to go to the pictures on a night. Farmers give them tweed suits, jackets and corduroy trousers so they don't stick out in a crowd. Most of them look very smart and the majority of them speak better English than we do. The Sergeant and Corporal might think that they're in the charge but really the prisoners have the run of a place.'

It was turning in much cooler on a night and there was a rumour that the prisoners weren't going to sleep in tents but would be moved into buildings. Where these buildings were, nobody knew. I went on seeing Achim as normal and but one night I had a date on with him so we all went down to meet them in the field as normal but when we got there, no tents. They had all gone.

'Ah well...' we all said.

That was it. It was fun knowing them. I'd known that it would eventually come to this: that they would be repatriated home, so I wasn't too upset although Mary and Joyce were pretty miserable.

'It is no good getting serious with these boys,' I told them, 'it is an adventure and when they go home, you will never hear from them.'

As far as I was concerned, I liked Achim, but if he went, then well it would be back to the dances for me. I told Mary and Joyce that I loved to dance. They were more for films, but after spending so many weeks together we got on well, so we arranged to meet up next weekend and all go to the Newcastle Cinema together. In the meantime, we couldn't stand in a field all night and it was too late to go to a dance, so we all went home.

'It'll be good for them if they've been sent home.'

I told my Mother when I got back and she agreed with me.

After two nights had passed, I came home from work as normal, had tea, got washed and got all poshed-up ready for a good night out with my friends. Pleated skirt, ankle-strap shoes, black stockings with seams up the back of them, my chiffon blouse with the bishop sleeves, gypsy earrings and a flashy bracelet, lipstick and powder with my hair in a long page-boy style. I was all done up and ready to go out when there was a knock on the door.

My Mother opened the door and I heard her say: 'Come in Achim.'

This was the first time Achim had come inside my home. They certainly were polite, the Germans; his manners were impeccable, not like a Geordie. He bowed, clicked his heels and there were flowers for my Mum.

Mum went off to make a pot of tea and I asked him:

'How did you get here? I thought you'd disappeared?'

Achim said, 'We have been moved to Hamsterley Hall.'

'Oh,' I said, 'I thought you'd been sent back home.'

'No Mary, not yet. Were you going out?' he asked.

'Yes, I was going to a dance,' I said.

Achim told me that there'd been a driver going from Hamsterley through to Rowland's Gill and so he'd asked the Sergeant if he could come and see me. The Sergeant had said yes, so he'd got a lift with the driver and then walked from Rowlands Gill to Winlaton, which is about five miles.

'It's not far,' he told me. 'We are in wooden huts on Lord Gort's estate, beside Hamsterley Hall.'

'Lord Gort has a medal for bravery,' I said.

'Yes, I know, we have met Lord Gort,' said Achim. Then he said, 'Mary, you can still come to see me. We will meet at Hamsterley Mill. There is a white cottage at the crossroads. Tell the other girls we will meet you there.'

I passed the message on to Joyce and Mary and we boarded the bus through Lockhaugh, along to Rowlands Gill and then past Lintzford to Hamsterley Mill. I'd never had any call to go to Lintzford or Rowlands Gill before, I'd always gone to films in Newcastle and my dances were all over the other side of the valley, so I'd nothing in common with Rowlands Gill or any of that area. It was a spooky place in the dark. The white house was just off the crossroads, one road going on to Hamsterley Colliery and the other road leading up Medomsley Bank to Consett.

Once we'd met up with Achim and the others, we decided to go for a walk, as the girls and I wanted to see Lord Gort's estate at Hamsterley. We walked back along the road to the entrance to Lord Gort's estate. At the bottom of the driveway was a small lodge, next to a sweeping drive with big wrought iron gates. There were woods everywhere and it was black dark, really black dark.

'You're certainly out of the way,' I told Achim.

Although it was dark, it was a lovely night and we were tripping ourselves up and giggling. Achim was a nice, decent man. He would keep asking how old I was. I was only eighteen but I'd fibbed and told him I was nineteen. He spoke very good English and was employed at the camp as an interpreter so he was no fool. I really liked him.

When we'd got to the top of the drive we saw Lord Gort's manor all lit up but it was getting late so I said, 'Girls, it's about time we were making our way back. I don't fancy walking home.'

We all walked back the way we'd come.

'Mary, I see you tomorrow?' asked Achim.

As it was Sunday afternoon, I agreed to meet him.

'It will be nice to see it in the daylight,' I said.

Chapter 17
A Trip to Sunderland

When I got back home my Mother said, 'Mary, you have had a visitor.'

'Who?' I asked her.

'Your penfriend, Jimmy Pratt,' she said. 'He's going to call back and see you.'

'Uh-oh...' I said.

My Mum said, 'I told him you were out somewhere so he's coming back one day this week.'

'Tomorrow afternoon I have a date on with Achim.' I told her. 'Maybe you should have said I was away working and wouldn't be back for months.'

'Now Mary, that young man was kind to you,' said my Mum. 'The least you can do is see him.'

'I never asked him to be kind,' I said. 'I never asked him for anything. He was just a penfriend and then he went and told his Mother that I was his girlfriend.'

Sunday came and I had my Sunday lunch as normal. After lunch, I washed my face and got ready to meet the girls and then we all went down to Hamsterley Mill to meet our young men.

'Actually,' I said to Mary and Joyce as we passed through Rowlands Gill and Lintzford, 'it's very nice here, quiet, green fields, woodlands'

It was. I met Achim and he said that he enjoyed the wood huts better than the tents.

'Much warmer too,' he said.

'Good,' I told him. 'A few months more in England and then home for you.'

Achim told me that he had written to his Mother for some photographs so that he could show me where he lived in Baden Baden, which he said was near the Black Forest.

We walked down to the cafe in Rowlands Gill and had ice cream and coffee. I was still full up from my Sunday lunch but I enjoyed the coffee. My Mother had made cold meat sandwiches. I knew that with coming to meet me, Achim would have missed his tea, so I gave him the sandwich box with my Mum's goodies in it and he said thank-you.

'I shall enjoy them,' he said. 'But we get plenty to eat in the camp.'

We all came home on the nine o'clock bus. We had arranged to meet the following weekend. Achim had told me that he sometimes went to Crook to do work.

'But Mary, if I can come through to you in the week then I will,' he said.

'Anytime,' I said.

Through the week though, Jimmy came back.

'My Mother would like to meet you,' he told me. 'I can come back and seek you on Saturday. Mrs Hymers, can I take Mary to meet my Mother next Saturday? I'll bring her back safe.'

'If you look after her,' my Mother told him, and Jimmy promised he would.

'See you on Saturday, Mary,' said Jimmy as he left.

When he'd gone, I said, 'Ma, I don't want to go.'

My Mum said, 'Mary. It is for one night and then that is it,' so I knew I didn't really have a choice.

The Saturday came and I saw Mary and Joyce and asked them to tell Achim that I couldn't make it that day.

'Will you tell him that I will see him through the week?' I asked them, and they promised that they would.

As I had promised, I went to Jimmy's home, but really, he was a stranger to me. All his relations and his Mother were very kind and she was immaculate in her home.

'You're our Jim's girlfriend then?' she said to me while I was helping her with the washing-up.

My heart was crying out, 'No!' But I didn't say

that to her.

Jimmy was a very kind and decent young man and I had written to him for quite a while when he was abroad, but "girlfriend" had never entered my head, in fact I'd never expected to even meet him.

I stayed the night and next morning I had my breakfast with Jimmy and his family before setting off back to Winlaton. Jimmy came back home with me and my Mum made tea for us.

On his way out the door, Jimmy said, 'Mary, I will come to see you again.'

I thought this was wrong. If I had had his home address then I could have told him, 'I'll write to you as a friend,' but I had no home address for him. I never thought to ask for it.

When Jimmy had left, my Mother said, 'No fancy?'

'No Mother, no fancy.' I told her. 'Still too young,' and I left it at that.

When I saw Achim later that week he asked, 'Why have you been away Mary?'

'I had to see a friend.' I said to him.

Whether he believed me or not I do not know but there was a glint in his eye which made me think, 'You do not believe me,' and if he didn't, then he was quite right not to.

We arranged to meet.

Achim said, 'Mary, they keep sending me to Crook.'

I said, 'That is a long way. What do you do over there?'

'Office work,' said Achim. 'I am an interpreter.'

He'd received some letters from home with photos. There was his Mother, she looked tall, rather nice and his Father too, very tall. But then so was Achim. He showed me a photograph of his sister too, he had only one sister. There was a very large house and driveway and with Achim being so well spoken I thought, 'It looks as if they're not short of a bob,' although all I said to him was, 'They look very nice.'

I got back to the house and the weekend arrived and with it my penfriend. When I heard the knock at the door, I said:

'Dad, go and tell him that I've moved to London.'

I knew my Father didn't like doing this. I know he did not like lying. He moved slowly to the door. Opened it.

I heard a voice ask, 'Is Mary in?'

Then I heard my Dad say, 'No, she's not in. She has gone to London. Her and her friend had the chance of a job down there.'

So, my penfriend walked away and I knew that was the finish.

My Father came back into the kitchen and said to me: 'Young lady, don't ever tell me to lie for you again. If you ever get into any problems then make sure to get yourself out of them yourself. Do not include me anymore. I doubt if you will hear from that young man again.'

Well for me, I breathed a huge sigh of relief and then I thought I would get dressed-up and go out. I had already promised Joyce and Mary that I would meet them and we'd all go to Rowlands Gill, probably to the cafe there for coffee and ice cream. We got there, and eventually made our way to Lintzford where we met our young men.

All of the men had shopping baskets and slippers with them and I asked, 'Who made these?'

They had made the baskets and the slippers out of thick raffia and decorated them with woven roses. They were really pretty and very well made.

'How much are they?' I asked.

'Ten shillings,' they said. 'Can you sell them?'

I promised to take some to work on the Monday and try to sell them to the girls I worked with.

Achim said to me, 'Mary, could we go to see a film one night?'

'Yes,' I told him, but then I asked, 'are you able to get out?' because I knew that there was a curfew on the camp and although they weren't prisoners of war because the war was over, they were still prisoners and if anyone had seen them in their uniform then they'd be in big trouble.

'I have a tweed jacket and corduroy trousers,' said Achim. 'I can go anytime to the pictures, so some night I shall come to your Mother's house and we will go out.'

'A date.' I said and he laughed.

I had known Achim for about six months by now and a couple of days later I came home from work, changed my clothes and was going to see a film when there was a knock at the door. I opened the door and I heard a voice say, 'Hello Mary, are you going out?'

It was Achim just like he'd promised.

'Yes', I said. 'I'm off to see a film. Would you like to come?'

Achim said he would love to see a film and my Mum made him a cup of tea and something to eat.

'How did you get here?' I asked.

'I got the bus to Rowlands Gill and then I have walked from there,' said Achim.

We walked down to Blaydon and got there for about seven o'clock. The big film was just beginning. The attendant had a torch in her hand and showed us to our seats. As we sat down, the ice-cream lady came round so I bought some ice cream. I knew that Achim did not have much money although the prisoners would sell a few paintings or slippers or shopping bags like the ones I took into the factory to sell for them. There were some very good artists among them. It was a lovely film and we both enjoyed it.

There were two shows a night and we had missed the little pictures at beginning of the film and so when the lights went on after the film had ended, we sat until the lights went out again and watched the cartoon and small film that we had missed at the start.

'Did you like the film?' I asked Achim when it was finished.

He said it was great.

'We'd better hurry and catch the next bus to Winlaton,' I said.

As we were coming out of the picture house, one or two people stopped to say hello to me and then there I was, sitting on the bus next to a tall, tanned young man. Well, Winlaton was a small village and everybody knew everybody but they certainly didn't know this young man. If they had done, then they'd have had something to talk about, what with him being a German prisoner of war. But I enjoyed his company; he was polite, well-spoken and decent and I liked that.

When we got back home, it was about nine-thirty and my Mother had made me some supper.

'It's a long walk to Rowlands Gill,' I told Achim. 'I'll walk you to Winlaton Mill and then the bus will take you along to Hamsterley Mill. Mum will you come and meet me on the way back as there's no houses past St Paul's Church and it's a bit dark?'

'We'll walk down to meet you,' my Dad promised.

After supper, off we went to the bus stop.

'Here's some money for your bus fare,' I said to

Achim but he told me:

'Mary, I have money, I shall get off at Hamsterley Mill. I have enjoyed my night.'

'Good.' I said.

'When will I see you again?' asked Achim and so we arranged to meet up again the next Saturday. I waited until his bus arrived and then saw my Mum and Dad waiting at the other side of the road.

'Well this is a surprise,' I said, as I linked them both.

There were houses at Winlaton Mill and their lights were twinkling as we walked away back up the fields. When we got home, we all finished off the night with a cup of tea and a great chunk of cake, then off to bed.

Chapter 18
A Stranger at the Door

The Sunday night after I'd gone to the pictures with Achim, I thought I would have a night in for a change. So when my Mum asked if I was going out, I said, 'Not tonight.'

About six o'clock, there was a knock on the door. My Father went to answer it and brought a young man back in with him.

'Mary, do you know this young man?' my Dad asked.

I looked at him and the young man said, 'Hello Mary.'

'Hello' I said, but I was dumbfounded. I had never seen this man before. Who was he?

'Well he evidently knows you,' said my Dad.

I looked at my Mother. Of course, whoever he was, we had to ask him to have a seat and as always Mum put the kettle on. I followed her into the kitchen.

'Who is he?' asked my Mum.

'I have never seen him before in my life,' I told her. 'How does he know who I am and where I live? His English is good though. Broken. But good.'

When we got back into the living room I said to him, 'Do I know you?'

'I know you,' he replied.

'How?' I asked.

'I know Achim,' he said.

'Oh,' I said.

The young man said his name was Helmut Rohmann and that he worked in the same office as Achim. Then he told me that Achim was going to be sent to Crook in Durham. I still didn't know why he had come to my house though. Helmut showed us photographs of his family; his Mother and Father. They looked like all Mums and Dads.

After a couple of hours, Helmut said that he was going back to the camp.

'Will you go for the bus?' I asked him.

'No,' Helmut said. ' I walk back to Hamsterley.'

'It's a very long walk from Winlaton,' I told him, but Helmut said that he didn't mind the walk.

I walked him to the back door, he shook my hand and went on his way.

'Very peculiar. Whatever made him come here?' asked my Mother.

She told me that Helmut had said to her: 'Mrs Hymers, would you let Mary marry a German?'

'Well what did you say?' I asked.

'I said that when Mary chooses to marry it will be Mary's decision. I have nothing to do with whom she chooses to marry.'

Thinking about it, I really think that Achim sent him, but I never said anything to Achim about Helmut visiting me and Achim never mentioned it.

The Saturday afternoon after Helmut had visited, Achim came to my Mother's house. Saturday was always a full house at my Mother's; in fact, Mum's house was always full of people. My Dad used to say, 'It's an open house, your Mum teas everyone.'

We were all gathered round the in the kitchen enjoying my Mother's cooking. She always put on a good spread: homemade cakes, home-baked bread, roast beef sandwiches thick with butter and mustard. My brothers were both in and my oldest brother, Alex, had brought his daughter Sandra along. We were all chatting away when the back door opened and I heard a voice say to my Dad, 'Is Mary in?' and my Dad saying, 'Yes,' and in walked a young chap in his Air Force uniform.

Once again I was amazed. It was Leslie the Airman. I'd been writing to him for the past three years, or rather my Mother had been writing to him for me, as I'd often been too busy to do it myself.

Leslie said hello to everyone and I introduced him to Achim. Achim was just about to shake his hand when Leslie looked at him and walked out of the house.

'Well that was quick,' said my Dad.

I laughed and said, 'Good.'

So that was rid of him.

When my brother Alex decided to go home, my little niece, Sandra, was in her pram so I wheeled her out the front door. Just as I was doing this, my brother said to me:

'Kid, where did you meet him?'

'He worked on the farm opposite.' I told him, 'Don't worry, he's just a friend.'

'He's the enemy,' said Alex but I just laughed.

'It's only a bit of fun,' I said. 'In any case, the War is over and there's no such thing as enemies, if there ever was anyway. Read your Bible.'

'Our Mary, you're nuts.' Alex said. 'He seems like a nice chap but you're young and daft.'

'Exactly,' I said.

After Alex went home, Achim and I went off to see a film. There were two shows on but we went early and came out at about quarter past eight so that Achim could get back to his camp. As Achim said, they had the run of the place. Their English was very good; in fact, they were better educated and better spoken than we were.

'I think that we shall be going home very soon,' said Achim.

'That's good,' I said.

'Promise you will write to me?' he asked and I promised that I would.

'My friend Karl would like to meet you' Achim told me. 'He is a very talented artist,' but I just said:

'Goodnight, I have to get back home. I'll see you tomorrow.'

We met the boys the next afternoon, which was Sunday.

When I saw Achim he said to me:

'Mary, They are going to send me to Crook, but I shall still see you. You can come to see me on the bus.'

Now Crook is in Durham, which is quite far from Winlaton, three hours each way, three buses each way.

'I don't think so,' I thought, but wasn't going to say that to Achim. Instead, I said:

'So this is goodbye or Auf Wiedersehen.'

'No Mary, we will find a way,' said Achim.

I thought to myself: 'Mary, it is impossible to see him at Durham. It is out of the question.'

'It is too far,' I said. 'I would have to board a bus to Durham then to Crook. Three hours. Three buses. No Achim. It is impossible. Goodbye. I hope it is not too long before you are home.'

Achim said, 'I shall write to you. I shall come back to see you.'

'We shall see,' I answered. 'It has been nice knowing you. Now the girls and I are going to walk back to Rowlands Gill as it is a lovely day.'

As I was leaving the house to meet Achim my Mum had said to me: 'I've made a few sandwiches for those boys. They'll probably miss their Sunday tea,' so I gave Achim the sandwiches and told him to share them amongst his friends.

As I walked back along to Rowlands Gill with Mary and Joyce, Joyce said to me:

'They are sending Achim to Crook. Are you broken hearted?'

'No,' I told them and then I said, 'You cannot get too serious with these chaps. Achim was nice and I enjoyed his company but to me it was adventure. Now I am back to my dancing at the Oxford.'

'We'll come along too,' said Mary and Joyce.

The next Saturday I was done up like a lop ready for my dance when there was a knock at the door. To my surprise, there stood Achim.

'I thought you'd gone to Crook?' I said.

'There was a lorry coming to Hamsterley so I asked permission if I could come to Hamsterley for the weekend' said Achim. 'The lorry driver is not going back to Crook until Monday.'

I knew that Joyce and Mary were still seeing their young men and so I got word through to them to tell them I had company.

'So how do you like Crook?' I asked Achim.

'It is not like Hamsterley. I cannot come and see my Mary,' he said.

I didn't answer him but I thought, 'Forget it.' There was no way that I was going to trail across to Crook.

Achim went back to Hamsterley for the night and came back the next day for his Sunday lunch and tea. When it was time for him to go back to Hamsterley, I told him:

'I shall walk you up past St. Paul's and then you can catch the bus at Winlaton Mill.'

During the walk, Achim told me that he would write to me if he could.

'We shall see each other again if someone is coming up to Hamsterley in an army lorry. This is the only way I can get to Hamsterley.'

'Auf Wiedersehen,' I told him and came back home.

During the week I received a letter from him to say that he was coming back up to Winlaton on the following Sunday. It was afternoon when he arrived at our house and he didn't leave until late that night.

'Achim, if we don't hurry, you'll miss your bus' I said, as we left the house.

Sure enough, some time after I'd got back from seeing him to the bus stop, there was a knock on the back door and there he was.

'Mary, I miss my bus,' he said as I opened the back door.

'Come in,' I said and we went back into the kitchen.

'Mrs Hymers I have missed my bus,' he told my Mum.

Of course my Mum told him that he could stay.

'You can sleep in Mary's bed tonight. Mary can sleep downstairs.'

'What time shall I wake you?' I asked Achim.

'What time do you get up Mary?'

'We rise at six' I said.

Our Norman came in from the pictures with his friends and by the time they had left, it was well past midnight so I said to our Norman, 'Show Achim to his bedroom.'

My Mum made a bed downstairs for me and the next morning at six o'clock I got up and got washed and dressed as usual before my Mum went up to wake Norman and Achim. We all sat down to breakfast and when I'd finished eating I asked Achim, 'Will you be all right? I have to go to work.'

'I will be all right Mary. I shall write to you. I cannot come to see you like I used to.'

'Don't worry about it' I said to him.

So I said cheerio to Achim. That was it. Two weeks passed and I got back into the swing of things, going to Newcastle to dance with my friends or to go to the pictures. Then I received a letter from Achim asking if I could meet him that night as he had the chance of a lift into Hamsterley for two hours.

Mary and Joyce came over to my house and we boarded the bus to Lintzford but when we got there, no Achim. Instead there was another young man waiting for us at the bus stop. He told me his name was Oscar and that the person who was supposed to have been driving the lorry for Achim to come to Hamsterley had been given another job to do instead and so Achim hadn't got a lift after all.

'Thank you for telling me,' I said. 'I know he is not free to do as he likes.'

'Well,' said Joyce. 'We can all go for a walk anyway.

As we walked from the bus stop I asked Oscar, 'Where were you captured?'

Oscar told me that he was a pilot and had been in the Mediterranean for four hours before he was picked up.

By now we'd reached the edge of the Hamsterley Estate and Joyce, Mary and I said that we were going to walk to Rowlands Gill. So all six of us walked along past Lintzford to Rowlands Gill. When we reached the edge of the village the Germans said that they weren't able to come any further.

'What a pity,' I said. 'We could all have called into the cafe for ice-cream and coffee.'

Instead we all said goodbye and the girls and I caught the bus back home.

Chapter 19
Goodbye to Achim

With Achim in Durham, I got back to my old friends and back to my old routine. Occasionally, Mary and Joyce came over to visit. About a week and a half after I'd met Oscar they called in one night after work and said to me:

'Mary, are you going anywhere special this weekend? Oscar would like to see you.'

I told them that I was going to the Picture House on Westgate Road with my friend Doreen as there was a good film on.

'I'll come with you next week,' I told them.

After the film, Doreen and I got off the bus in Blaydon and sat on the church wall for a while. On Sunday nights, the Salvation Army played in Blaydon Square and although I'd heard them many times, they had a great band and the atmosphere was good.

But then there was always a good atmosphere then. We were all brought up to be mannerly. We said please and thank-you. If you got on a bus, a young man would always stand up to give you his seat. We were taught to be polite and to have dignity, to be open with one another and not to have secrets. We listened to our hymns too and were always good attenders at St Paul's Church on a Sunday. If you managed a full years attendance at Church you were given a nice bible or hymn book with your name on it. I kept mine for years but as the years dwindled by they got old and worn until they couldn't be kept any longer. Of course religion was always something that fascinated me; why are we here? But wondering about religion didn't stop me getting on and enjoying my life.

The next weekend, Joyce and Mary arrived to seek me.

'Have you heard from Achim?' they asked.

'I've had two letters,' I told them. 'But it is difficult for him to come to Hamsterley as the Army lorries don't come this way. Anyway, I'm not going to live my life waiting for Achim. These boys are going home. There's no way I'm going to take it seriously. It's just a good friendship. Achim thinks that I am nineteen but I'm only eighteen and a half and this is a time to have fun. I am pleased I have known him but that is it.'

I went back to Hamsterley with Joyce and Mary and met up with Oscar again. He spoke good English.

'Mary,' he said. 'Mary, why you did not come last week?'

'I was in Newcastle with my friend. We went to see a film,' I told him. 'Were you really in the sea for four hours?'

'Yes. An English ship picked me up in the Mediterranean.'

'And now you are in Hamsterley meeting Mary Hymers,' I said.

'Yes, Mary,' said Oscar. 'But I have seen you many times with Achim.'

'Well, there was nothing to it,' I told him. 'It was just a friendship. When you all go home you will be able to go out with your own girls and this will be like a dream.'

'Achim likes you Mary,' said Oscar, 'and he also likes your Mother and Father. He said you were very kind.'

'My Mother is kind to everyone and she never objects to who I go out with,' I told Oscar. 'I can please myself and do what I like and I do.'

'Then will you come next Saturday and see me again?' Oscar asked.

'Yes,' I said. 'I shall come over with Joyce and Mary.'

We all said goodnight and came home. As usual over supper I told my Mother where I'd been and about this young man, Oscar.

My Mother really did let me please myself about

what I did. She knew my character very well and that if I got fed-up then that would be it with Mary Hymers. I was really happy-go-lucky and if people did not like my style? Tough luck.

I said to my Mother:

'He seems a nice young man and I am meeting him again next Sunday.'

I was on my way to bed when my baby brother Norman came in. He looked very smart in his black suit with white shirt and a tie.

I clocked the outfit and asked him:

'Who's the girlfriend?'

Our Norman laughed:

'I'm not so daft,' he said. 'They're far from my mind.'

Monday, Tuesday, Wednesday went by. Thursday night I came home from work and Achim was sitting having tea with my parents.

'Hello,' I said when I saw him.

He didn't smile.

'Mary,' he said, 'I turn my back for two or three weeks and you have another boyfriend.'

'Well,' I said. 'I have no explanation for you.'

'I cannot come back to see you like I used to' Achim told me.

I said to him:

'Achim you are on your way back home and this

will be forgotten.'

He turned to my Mother and Father.

'Mr and Mrs Hymers, you have been very kind to me and I thank you for your kindness.'

But he never said anything else to me and walked out.

'Well,' My Mum said to me. 'You have hurt that young man's feelings,' and she laughed at me. 'Don't you care?'

'No, not really,' I told her and so that was the end of that.

Chapter 20
Oscar

Saturday came around once again and my Mother and I went to Newcastle to look for a new dress for me. We got off the bus at Marlborough Crescent and I linked arms with her as we walked up through Clayton Street. We had a great time looking in the different shops but there was nothing there I liked so I thought we would go to C&A Modes. C&A's was a huge clothes shop that sold everything: men's suits, children's clothes. It practically catered for all your needs.

Once we were inside, I got my eye on this pinafore dress. It was rather nice. Chocolate brown, it had a bibbed front with crossover straps that fastened at the back and a lovely flared skirt. We bought the pinafore and then started to look for a blouse or jumper to wear underneath it. I saw a pink angora jumper I quite liked. It was nice and fluffy so we bought that too. My shoes were a court shoe and were tan and went with the outfit.

After I had got my outfit, my Mother wanted to do some shopping, so we went down to the Grainger Market where she bought her veg and rabbits and some hock to cook with the rabbits. Then we walked up to the Haymarket and called into the pork shop and bought pork sandwiches, pease pudding and black pudding. The black pudding was to be cooked in with the rabbits as well. She got my Father and Gradfather's favourite supper too: pigs trotters, along with some tripe, so we were really loaded with shopping coming home.

By the time we got back home it was tea-time, so we had some ham sandwiches along with some of Mum's home-cooked cakes. When I'd finished, it was time to get ready for the dance. I got washed and poshed-up: earrings, lipstick and powder, then dressed in my new outfit, off I went to Blaydon Church Hall with my friends. I got lots of dances and a couple of polite: 'Can I take you home's?' from some of the boys there, to which my answer was always a firm, 'No!'

It was an eleven o'clock finish at the dance and my friends and I came out and started to walk back along to St Cuthbert's Church. As we walked along past the Church, there was my brother Norman and his pals Ginger and Wilf sitting on the Church wall.

'Goodnight boys,' I said as I passed them and they all said 'Goodnight.'

Then my brother Norman shouted after me:

'Tell Ma I'm hungry. Tell her I want something nice for supper!'

'I will' I said, but we had only got halfway up Blaydon Bank when Norman ran up after us and we all walked home together.

It was nearly midnight when we got home and as soon as we entered the house, Mum was on with the kettle. She was always there waiting for us. On the table was a feast and of course we were all good at eating. I have always in my life carried on my Mother's recipe for eating well.

'Never build a castle on bad foundations,' she'd say and her table was always fit for a King.

After supper, we all went up to bed. I put my curlers in and slept like a log until the morning. What with all the exercise we took: dancing, walking, working, we never had any trouble sleeping.

Sunday morning was my lie-in and I usually didn't get up until 8 o'clock. By then my Mother was already up baking and preparing Sunday lunch. I always asked if I could help her and always got the answer: 'No. I am all done and only finishing off.'

At twelve on the dot, lunch was served. After she'd cleared up lunch was the only time Mum got a rest. She would have a snooze on the armchair. My Mother never stopped, God love her. My Grandfather was now well into his eighties and he still struggled up from the Burn to my Mother's to eat at our house. Mum looked after her youngest brother Joseph, my Uncle Joe too. She would go down to Blaydon Burn every day with their lunch and shopping, after she'd trailed up the Street and back to get it. It was a two-mile round trip so, to help my Mother, when I was off work, I would go down to my Grandfather's and tidy the home for them.

At four o'clock, I met Joyce and Mary and we caught the bus to Rowlands Gill and then walked from the Gill to Lintzford. It was about two miles but the sun was shining and it was a lovely walk.

When we got nearer to Lintzford there were four young men coming to meet us: Oscar, Richard, Helmut and another other young man, Johnny Thones, who had come from Luxembourg. We said hello to each other and then decided to walk through Lord Gort's estate. It was woodlands and green fields and the sun shone, although, if it had rained, there was a bridge where we could shelter. Oscar would ask me where I had been through the week.

'Dancing, films,' I would say.

I think it must have been awfully boring for them in the camp. Of course they worked on the farms and were probably glad to rest on a Saturday or Sunday but there wasn't that much for them to do, as they didn't have much money.

Oscar asked me if Achim had come to see me and I told him that he had.

'He wondered why I had gone out with you. He was not very pleased with me,' I told him. 'I was going to explain to him when he was at my Mother's but he didn't give me a chance. I was going to say to him, 'Oscar came to tell me that you had gone to Crook. This is how I met him.'

'We are all going home,' said Oscar.

'Of course you are,' I replied. 'This is what I mean. We are all good friends and we have a nice time together, but you won't be here forever.'

'No,' said Oscar. 'Helmut and Richard are being moved to London before being sent home. This is the last time Mary and Joyce will see them.'

We walked back to Lintzford. I went on ahead with Oscar and Johnny, while Helmut and Richard said their goodbyes to Joyce and Mary.

'We will meet next week?' asked Oscar.

'Bring Joyce with you,' said Johnny.

'I shall ask her,' I said.

When we left them I said to Joyce and Mary:

'Eventually they will be moving them all home, once the Government gets round to it. But it was nice meeting someone different.'

Then I said to Joyce:

'That young man who was with Oscar would like to meet you.'

'Oscar told me he liked you,' Joyce told me.

'Joyce,' I said. 'I meet Oscar and we have a good laugh but I take everything with a pinch of salt. I do not take any of it seriously.'

'Are you seeing Oscar again?' Joyce asked me.

I told her that he'd asked me to meet him through the week.

Joyce said:

'Well Mary, I shall come along with you and meet Johnny. Helmut says that he is going to write to me but it won't last long because I do not like writing letters. We'll maybe have a few but it will die off. As you say Mary: out of sight, out of mind.'

'How is Achim?' asked Mary.

I told them that he'd come to my Mum's and told me off in a very polite sort of way for going out with Oscar while he was in Crook.

'Anyway,' I said, 'come to my house on Wednesday Joyce, and when I come from work we will go across and see them.'

Oscar and I met three times a week. Once I met him and it was pretty chilly, so he was wearing his Air Force uniform. He had his overcoat on. A heavy coat. It looked very warm and reached down to his ankles. He looked very smart but what he said to me was:

'Mary, the English think their uniforms are really good.'

'I don't think our boys think they are good uniforms,' I replied. 'They prefer their civilian clothes.'

'In any case, Oscar,' I told him. 'It is not the uniform; it is the gentleman who wears the uniform and what kind of heart he has that matters.'

So there was no more said about uniforms.

Another time, he said to me:

'My brother has been captured in Russia. I will be going home shortly but my brother will not. He will be sent to Siberia.'

'That's very sad,' I said, but I really felt like saying: 'You started it.' But I didn't. Instead I thought: 'Mary keep your mouth shut or you could start another war.'

It was nice to meet the enemy. They were all decent young men. Their manners were out of this world. On meeting you, they would click their heels and bow when you were introduced to them. This really fascinated me. A Geordie would never do that and that was why I was never interested in a Geordie boy. They were more rough and tumble. Don't get me wrong. I'm British, body and soul, and I knew some nice young men. But I never courted an Englishman.

They were pretty clever at making things too: shopping bags, slippers, Perspex hearts and brooches you could put a photo in. I sold them at my work for them and a lot of people bought them. They were very well spoken with good English as well, especially Oscar and Achim. I often wondered about our education when I thought of them.

Achim, I think, was a different class to us. I could imagine that he'd had a good education. He was an interpreter and his English was very, "What, what" and proper, but I never took our dating seriously. Don't get me wrong. I did like him. He was a gentleman and he respected me. Oscar too. I liked him as well.

Sometimes, I would ask Oscar about the Belsen Concentration Camp and the Gas Chambers and he would say: 'Mary, I never heard of them.'

We all used to say: 'So they all say!' But maybe they never did hear of them. They could have been speaking the truth. They had been in a different part of the world, trying to win the war just as we had. They were the enemy but I got to know them and they were human.

Chapter 21
The First Dance

The weeks passed by and it was dances, films, and going out. We never stayed in. Once in a while, I would have an early night, wash my hair and go to bed at about nine o'clock, but it was rare when that happened. On those nights I would sleep very well. It was all the exercise, the dancing, and the long walks. You were never afraid to walk anywhere then.

Oscar had been sent back home and I received a letter from him every week, sometimes two. He said that jobs were hard to get, and he told me that as soon as he got settled at home he would send for me to come to Germany. I knew, but did not tell him, that Mary would never venture there. But I thought that eventually, he would meet one of his own girls and that would be it.

Months went by until one Saturday night, Doreen and my friends decided to go to Rowlands Gill dance. The dance had an eleven o'clock finish and by the time we had walked back from Rowlands Gill to Winlaton it would be nearing midnight. But there were five of us going and if it was a moonlit night we would enjoy the walk home. So I told my Mother that I would be home by midnight, and she asked who I was going with.

'Doreen and the girls,' I told her.

Saturday night came and we all got dressed up. I'd seen Doreen that morning and she'd asked what I was wearing.

'I have a black taffeta skirt with loads of material in it, my blue chiffon blouse with the bishops sleeves and my seamed stockings and ankle-straps' I told her. I had a royal blue short coat and matching earrings and bracelets too.

'I'll dress the same' she said.

The dance started at seven o'clock. We had caught the bus that got us to the Gill for about seven-thirty. It was only a short walk from the bus stop to the dance hall. There were only a few people in the hall when we arrived but that didn't matter because Doreen was a good dancer and we had the floor pretty much to ourselves.

By eight-thirty, the hall started to fill up. About forty young men came in all at once and stood together in one corner of the room. After a few dances, one came across to me and bowed.

'Dance?' he said.

That was his only word. So of course I danced with him and when the dance ended, he brought me back to my seat.

'Who's that?' asked Doreen.

'I don't have a clue' I told her. 'They look foreign to me.'

'He bowed' said Doreen.

'Yes, that's what makes me think he's not English' I said.

Doreen and I had a few more dances together and then he came back again, bowed and we danced again.

'Kosta' he said, and so I gathered that was his name.

'Mary' I told him, and we kept on dancing.

Later during the dance, two more young men came into the Hall. One of them had sleek wavy hair.

'I kind of like him,' I thought to myself.

I knew he was not English. He didn't look English. But he was good-looking and I thought he would not find it difficult to find a girl.

The other young man he came in with looked carefree. I noticed that he got a girl up for a dance and so I watched him dancing. My type. He was great. He swirled this girl around the room. Then Kosta came back and asked me to dance again. He was a good-looking chap. His hair, any girl would have been envious of that mop of hair. It was full of ringlet that fell over his face and he seemed like a nice chap. But his dancing! He was so stiff.

By now I was standing next to the chap with sleek black wavy hair and I heard a young girl say to him: 'Hi Romeo.'

'A-ha,' I thought. 'He looks that type.'

Romeo's friend came up to me and bowed. His English was very broken.

'Would you like to dance?' he asked.

I said I would. As I had seen, he was a great dancer and could swirl you around the dance floor.

By now it was nearly home time, in fact, it was the last dance and Kosta came back across to me. He took hold of my hand and as far as I could make out, he said:

'Monday – Newcastle – Pictures.'

I had my watch on and pointed to my watch. Six o'clock? He nodded and off he went.

'Peculiar' I thought. 'Another foreign man.'

But Kosta was not my type so I thought: 'I hope he does not come on Monday night.'

We'd decided not to walk back home after all but instead take a taxi to Winlaton. The next day Doreen came over to my Mum's house and asked:

'Mary, those lads at the dance last night, who are they?'

'I haven't a clue,' I told her.

Doreen didn't stay long. She had met an English man at the dance and she'd set a date on with him for that night, so after a cup of tea she went back home to get ready.

'I'll see you back at work on Monday,' I said to her as she left.

I'd already told my Mother all about meeting Kosta who couldn't speak English, after the dance on Saturday, so on Monday morning I said to her:

'Don't make any tea for me tonight, Mum, I'm meeting Kosta and we're going to the pictures. I hope he is not there, but I shall go in case he is. I do not want to make a fool of him if he comes all the way from Rowlands Gill.'

I finished work at five o'clock as normal and washed my face and added some more powder and lipstick in the toilets there. I was already dressed to go out. I had time for a cup of tea so I walked down to Mark Toney's and had some coffee and iced cakes. By the time I'd finished, it was time to go to Marlborough Crescent and see if Kosta had come in on the Consett bus. There he was standing waiting for me so I went over and said hello.

'We shall go and see a film,' I told him, but I don't think he knew what I was talking about. We went to the Essoldo and saw a nice film.

'Where do you live?' I asked him.

'Hamsterley Hall,' said Kosta.

'Oh, I know that very well,' I told him, but he didn't understand me.

'Shall I take you to your bus?' I asked him.

'I see you?' asked Kosta.

I understood.

'Dance, Saturday night,' I told him.

He nodded. That was it. No Saturday night dance for Mary.

After I put Kosta on the bus back to Rowlands Gill, I caught my own bus and came home. I was starved hungry and dying for a cup of my Mother's tea. I got home for ten o'clock.

'You're home quick,' my Mother said.

'He's from Hamsterley Hall' I told her. 'No more. He told me he'd see me at the dance on Saturday, so there'll be no Mary going to Rowlands Gill for a few weeks. It will be the Oxford on Saturday night with the girls.'

'Did you not like him?' asked my Mum.

'If you'd seen his ringlets,' I said to her. 'He seemed like a nice chap, nice looking but not my type. He'll find another girl. In any case, I have rather taken a fancy to this Romeo.'

'If he is a Romeo,' said my Mum.

'As soon as he entered the dance hall, something clicked inside me,' I told her. 'Even though I only saw him once.'

After few weeks went by, I thought it was probably safe to go back to Rowlands Gill dance on a

Saturday night, so off we all went. The band was a good one with an accordion, piano, saxophone, and drums.

We paid our two shillings to get into the dance and then went into the cloakroom and gave the cloakroom lady tuppence for her to look after our coats until the end of the dance. There were ladies toilets in the cloakroom too and mirrors so we could fix our hair and put some more war paint on: lipstick and powder. We were young and gorgeous – at least we thought so.

When we went into the dance hall, the lights were on and it was warm and everything looked nice and cosy. It got pretty crowded as the night wore on, but it was still quite early and as before the dance hall was fairly empty, so Doreen and I were the first on the dance floor. As we danced, the Hall began to fill up. After the first two dances, the lights would come on full, and you could really see who was in the dance hall. During the dances, the lights were dimmed, and there was a silver ball on the ceiling, which would slowly turn, and the beams would light up the dance-floor.

We danced for a bit and then Doreen and I thought we would have a cup of coffee and a chocolate éclair. We had our coffee and cakes, which I really enjoyed as I am a sweet tooth and they were thick of cream, and we were chatting to everyone who was taking a break.

When we'd finished eating we got a few more dances from different lads and then, just like the last time, these young men came in again and stood in a corner. But after a few minutes, this one good-looking man came across and bowed. I'd liked him a few weeks ago and here he was again.

He was pretty thickset in build. No tie. His shirt had no collar. Navy pinstriped suit. His hair was immaculate, deep waves. His trousers were razor-edged, very well creased. I thought he looked a bit Gypsy, in fact, I thought he looked like a Don Juan. He spoke. Bowed. I gathered he wanted to dance.

As I was dancing with him, I thought: 'I liked you the first time I saw you come into the dance hall.'

Peculiar but it was true. I had liked him from the first time I saw him.

When we'd finished dancing and had gone back to where we had been standing, Doreen asked:

'Who is that Mary?'

While we'd been having our coffee and cakes, I'd listened to what some of the other girls were saying about the foreign lads.

'I think they are from the camp at Hamsterley Hall,' I said. 'I think they've been in the concentration camps in Germany.'

'He's taken a fancy to you,' she said.

Just then though, a young lady came into the hall and making straight for Romeo, she said:

'Romeo, where is Chris?'

He said something in his own language to this other chap standing with us, the one who was such a good dancer. His name was Karl. Karl had better English than the rest of them and said, 'Daisy, Chris come later on.'

Just as Karl said that, another man came into the dance hall. He was about six foot and Daisy shouted: 'Chris!' and ran towards him and after that the pair of them stuck together all night.

The night wore on and this Romeo didn't leave my side. I danced with him all night. Doreen had also met a young man and at the end of the dance, she came up and suggested that we got a cab back home so it was time to say goodbye. When the taxi arrived, Romeo took hold of my hand and would not let it go.

'Tomorrow,' he said, but I told him:

'No. I go to dance,' and I pointed back at the dance we had been to.

'Sunniside Church Hall,' I said.

'Church dance?' he said and I nodded.

'Dance tomorrow night. Church first.' Then I said:

'Guten Nacht Romeo.'

'Tony.' he said.

I pointed to me. 'Mary,' I told him.

He still had a hold of my hand.

'Dance?' he asked.

I nodded, 'At Sunniside,' and he understood.

'Sprechen Sie Deutsch?' he asked.

I laughed and said, 'Nein' but thought: 'Their German must be good.'

I took my hand away and got into our taxi and home we came.

Chapter 22
A Late Night

My Mother was waiting for us when we got back. She would never go to bed until we were all home. She had made me porridge with warm milk and cream to pour over the top and there was cold meat and beetroot waiting for when Norman got in. This was late at night and I could have had meat too if I'd wanted it, but my Mother knew that I liked sweet.

'It's better for bed-time,' she would say.

I told her my news, everything that had happened that night.

'Do they never ask Doreen out?' my Mother asked.

'No. Isn't it peculiar? She gets the Englishmen; I get stuck with a foreigner.'

'What's he like then?' my Mum said.

I said:

'This Daisy called him Romeo but he told me his name was Tony. He seems nice and he's very good-looking.'

'Stay clear of him,' said my Mother, 'If they call him Romeo, he must know plenty of young girls.'

'I wonder why they have come here? I said to her. 'They do not understand English. I know they've come into this country from the Prisoner of War camps in Germany but fancy ending up in Rowlands Gill. It's peculiar too that I first saw Romeo at the dance a few weeks ago but I only danced with that Kosta. But Romeo, I mean Tony, was standing beside the doorway and as soon as I laid eyes on him something clicked inside me, but I let it pass. Now I see him again and he was with me for every dance and followed me to the taxi. He wanted me to go to a film. I tried to make him understand I'd be at the dance at Sunniside. But who they are, what they are and why they are here, I do not know.'

My brother Norman arrived back in the house just as I finished eating; he had been to the Miners Dance Hall. I had never known him to take a girl out; he was more of a rugby man, and he liked a drink. But by now it was well past midnight and we were all tired so we went up to bed.

I always slept well, right into Sunday morning and I got out of bed at around eight-thirty and put my curling pins in. I made a silk scarf into a turban around my head to keep them in; all the girls did that to keep their curlers in place. When I went downstairs I offered to tidy up for my Mother, but she said:

'No, I'll do it, it's your weekend off, enjoy,' so I went to see Doreen.

Doreen had a date with her boyfriend but she was going to the Sunniside dance too and meeting him inside the hall, so we arranged to travel up together, along with Sadie and Elsie who were also going.

'What's happening with Tony?' Doreen asked.

'He wanted me to go see a film at Rowlands Gill,' I told her, 'but I said that I was going to the dance, so we're meeting at the dance instead.'

I got back from Doreen's in time for my Mother's Sunday lunch and then had a restful afternoon before starting to get all dressed-up for my night out. What to wear? I put on my chocolate brown pinafore dress with a tan blouse, shoes, and earrings, and went off to meet my friends before we all went to Church.

After the Mass, the Reverend Father was at the door when we left and he said to everyone:

'Enjoy the dance. I shall see you in the Hall.'

So off we went into this Church Hall. It was a small band and there were quite a few inside already. We took off our coats and went into the cloakroom to do our faces a bit more and then we walked into the dance and there was Romeo, or to give him his proper name, Tony because it was the girls who had christened him Romeo.

He was with a few of his friends from the camp, including Karl who got me up a few times for different dances. What a dancer. Exactly my type. I thought to myself: 'I like Tony's dancing, but Karl is so light on his feet he can buzz you around.'

Karl had his eye on a young lady too, a very smartly dressed girl with very long hair done in the Veronica Lake style. I knew her name was Bette Jack but I didn't know her that well.

Between two of the dances, I asked Tony, 'Where do you live?' and hoped that he would understand me. He didn't.

Karl and Tony spoke to each other in their own language. Tony's face lit up and he put his arm around me.

'Hamsterley Hall,' said Karl.

Tony repeated: 'Hamsterley Hall.'

'Oh my God. Not again,' I thought.

Karl's English was not good but it was understandable.

'Where have you come from?' I asked.

He was babbling what I was saying back to Tony and Tony was babbling back to him, and then Karl said:

'We have been in Prisoner of War Camps in Germany for all the war.'

'Oh,' I said. 'Why did you come to this country?'

'We had a choice. Australia, America or England

and we came to England.'

He was translating everything to Tony as I spoke.

'Why England?' I asked.

'It is nearer home,' Karl replied.

'Why did you not go back home?'

'It is occupied by Russia and we will not go back under Russian rule. Tony wants to know where you live,' Karl said.

I told him I lived in Winlaton.

'He would like to take you home,' said Karl.

I said: 'Tell him that I have two buses to catch: one at Rowlands Gill and another to Winlaton, and as his English is really not good then he would get lost.'

Well he told Tony this and Tony laughed and spoke to Karl for a moment. Then Karl said to me:

'Tony says to tell you, I take Mary to Rowlands Gill and to tell her that I will see her tomorrow night at seven o'clock.'

After that, we danced until it was time to go home. Doreen had her boyfriend with her and so we all got the bus to Rowlands Gill together. Of course Tony had his arm through mine as we walked to the bus stop.

'Do not lose your bus,' I told him.

'Tomorrow, Mary' Tony said.

'Seven o'clock' I said.

But of course we had all talked and loitered so much that by the time we got to the bus stop we'd missed our bus back to Winlaton Mill.

'We'll have to walk it,' I told them, 'I'll not get home till very late.'

I must have looked a bit upset because Tony said something to Karl and then Karl spoke to me:

'Tony says not to be worried. You come back to camp with us and we get you home'

So Doreen and her young man, Karl, and Tony and me walked along from Rowlands Gill to Hamsterley.

As we got to the Gatehouse at the entrance to the Estate, Karl put his fingers on his lips.

'You must be quiet now,' he told us, so Doreen and I stopped talking.

The gates to the camp were shut tight.

'You wait here,' said Karl, and the three of us stood beside the gates as Tony and Karl climbed over them, very quietly.

We waited for about ten minutes and then Doreen said to me: 'Do you think they've left us Mary?'

'I hope not' I said to her. 'It's a longer walk back to Winlaton from here than it is from the Gill and I'm already late home. But they might have been caught by the Commandant and not be able to get out again. Let's give them five more minutes and then we'd better walk.'

Just as I said that, the gates started to swing open

and there was Tony and Karl and about ten other lads pushing this army truck through the gates. They were trying so hard to be quiet they were practically pushing it on tiptoe. They pushed it right past us onto the road. Karl pointed for Doreen and her young man to get into the back of the truck and Tony and I got into the front with the driver who was called Ziggy. It was a bit of a squeeze with three of us in the front. Karl and the rest started to push the truck down the road again and when it was going quite fast the engine suddenly started and some of the ones that were pushing jumped into the back of it while the rest of them disappeared back into the Camp. As we drove through the Gill there were a few lights went on at the sound of a truck rolling past so late but we got to Lockhaugh without seeing a soul.

The drive was a bit jerky because Ziggy was quite short and the only way he could reach the pedals and the steering wheel was to have the seat pulled right forward and to sit on an orange box and to work the pedals he'd slide off the box and then get back on again quick. But when we got to Stampy Moss Bank, the seat suddenly went backwards really quickly and he fell off the box onto the floor. One moment he was on the seat and then the next moment, he was on the floor under the driver's seat with the orange box on top of him. He tried to get back on the seat but every time he did, he hit the accelerator or the brake so the truck was either going really fast or nearly stopping.

'You're going to die, Mary,' I thought, but I got the

giggles and couldn't stop.

Tony and everyone in the back of the truck were all shouting, 'Shush,' at me but they were all giggling too. Eventually though, Tony managed to grab Ziggy's arm and pulled him back up onto his seat and we got up the bank and drove past St Paul's into Winlaton.

When we got about half-way down North Street, I said to Ziggy, 'You stop here,' because I didn't want my Mother to know that I'd come home in a stolen truck. When the truck stopped, I turned to Tony,

'I go home now,' I told him, and got out of the truck.

Tony followed me out of the truck and as I got down I saw that Doreen and her young man and Karl had got out of the back of the truck too. Tony took my arm and said something to Karl.

'Tony says he will walk you to your house,' said Karl.

We walked down North Street until we got to my house and I opened the gate and started to walk down the path. Just as I reached the front door, it opened and my Mum reached out and grabbed me by the elbow.

'You. Inside now,' she said and dragged me inside. Then she looked at Tony and said to him, 'You're far too good-looking. You'll break her heart,' and shut the door.

It was nearly one.

'You missed the bus then,' she said.

'We did,' I said, and while I had my supper, I told her all about them stealing the truck to get us home.

'We danced all night,' I said. 'His English is terrible but he will learn.'

'What about Doreen?' my Mother asked.

'I think she is goofy-eyed with her young man,' I told her.

'Why do they call him Romeo?' my Mum asked.

I laughed. 'He looks like a Romeo. But don't worry, Mum. I thought I would not appeal to him but seemingly I have. I could not move for him. It will probably wear off. Just a fling.'

Monday night came. I came home from work, got ready for my date and said to my Mum:

'Will you come and meet me at Winlaton Mill at about ten-thirty please? I don't want to walk those fields back myself.'

'I'll be there. Me and your Dad,' My Mum said.

'Actually, Mum,' I told her, 'I might be home sooner if he cannot understand me. I'm still debating whether or not to go. If I'm not home by nine o'clock come and meet me.'

My Mother told me again that they'd meet me and I left the house and went for the bus.

I boarded the bus for Rowlands Gill, got off at the bus stop, and there was Tony waiting for me. We went to see a film. It was about ten o'clock when we came out. I tried to make him understand English. It was hard work.

'Tony, I must go for my bus,' I said.

' I see you tomorrow night?' Tony asked, but I shook my head.

'No,' I told him. ' Not tomorrow. Dance Saturday night,' and Tony repeated what I'd said.

The week passed but we were out every night; Church Hall dances, films at the Oxford, and so the days went by very quickly until it was Saturday night again.

Doreen and I were always early for our dances as that way you could move around the dance floor until it got more crowded. Then I saw Tony and Karl come in and of course they both came over as soon as they saw us. Karl's was still the better English but Tony's English was improving a little now and after we'd said hello, he said to me:

'We go to Newcastle tomorrow?'

'Yes,' I told him. 'We shall go to the Westgate Picture house. There's different variety acts on, on a Sunday night.'

'We go?' he asked again.

'Yes,' I told him, but I was thinking; 'If it comes out early I shall take him home and let my Mum see who I am going out with.'

I said to Karl, 'Tell him in your own language that I shall meet him at Marlborough Crescent.'

Karl spoke to him and then said back to me, 'He

says he does not know where that is,' so I said to Karl:

'Tell him it is the bus stop in Newcastle and that he's to stay in the same place when he gets off the bus and I will find him.'

Karl must have told him because Tony said, 'Alright, Mary.'

'Good. Your English is getting better' I told him.

On Sunday night, I thought I would put on my new coat to meet Tony. It was a chocolate brown swing coat with a half-belt at the back and I wore it with my light tan shoes and brown kid gloves. Before I left the house, I said to my Mother:

'Expect company tonight, I shall bring Tony home after we have been to Newcastle to see the variety show.'

'Good,' said my Mum.

I got the bus into Marlborough Crescent and there he was standing, waiting for me. He looked rather nice. He was wearing a military white mackintosh and his hair was in deep waves. He was very well groomed. Crisp shirt and razor-edge creases in his trousers; they were so sharp I think he must have sewn a seam down them with a machine to keep them like that. He was nice. Good-looking. Yes. I really was eyeing him up and I could not find a fault. But who was he? Where was he from? I put my arm through his and said, 'Hello. You found your way then.'

'Where we go?' he asked. His English really was

getting better.

I said, 'We go to Mark Toney's for ice-cream.'

'Are you hungry?' he asked.

'No,' I told him. 'We go there until the show opens.'

I changed my mind about where we were going and, instead of the Westgate picture house, we went to the Essoldo instead. We came out at about nine o'clock.

'Not go home yet, Mary.' Tony said.

I said, 'No. You come to my house.'

We walked back to my bus stop and we waited for the bus. It was terrible really the way I was still trying to find fault with him. But standing at the bus stop with him, in looks and stature I could find no fault. He was really what I looked for in a man. A film star on a movie screen could not compete with him.

The Winlaton bus came in and I said, 'I'll get the bus-fare Tony.' Of course my fare was nothing as I had a three-month bus pass but I got his fare, as they were still confused about English money. When we got back to Winlaton, I said 'We shall call into my Mum's for a cup of tea.'

When we got to my house, my Mother was expecting us and as always, there was plenty to eat. He bowed as I introduced him saying: 'How do you do, Mother.'

My Mother liked that and said: 'I'll make you a

cup of tea, Tony.'

My Father was at home and he asked Tony where he was from.

'Riga, Latvia.'

'Is Tony your name?' my Dad asked.

'No,' said Tony. 'My name is Teofilius Anton Yakubovskis. Everyone calls me Tony for short.'

'It's nearly ten-thirty,' I said. 'We should be careful not to miss your bus, it's quite a walk to your camp so we best go.'

I walked him to the bus stop and when the bus arrived, I said to the Conductoress:

'When he gets to Rowlands Gill as he's not sure of the road, will you set him right?'

'Don't worry,' the Conductress told me. 'I shall put him off at Rowlands Gill.'

'I'll be alright, Mary,' said Tony, 'I see you tomorrow night?'

'I will see you Wednesday night,' I said.

'I meet you at my place, Wednesday night,' said Tony. 'I meet you at the bus stop. There is a film in camp and accordion playing too.'

When I got back into the house, I said to my Mother:

'Do you approve?'

'He looks fast,' she said. 'Like Don Juan.'

I told her that the first time I saw him something

clicked inside me.

'I can't explain it,' I told her.

'Well honey, you're very good at changing your mind,' my Mum said.

Chapter 23
A Trip to Scotland

When Wednesday night came, I rushed back from work, had my tea, tidied myself up, and changed from my work clothes into something more glamorous. Then off I went to meet Tony.

When I got to Rowlands Gill, Tony was waiting for me at the bus stop and we walked back to the camp at Hamsterley. They had a big hall with a volleyball court and a stage where there were also small tables and chairs. There was exercise kit and a boxing ring so they could keep fit. They had a large garden too and in the centre of the garden was a mosaic of the Latvian flag, which they had made by gathering small stones and painting them.

'I will show you where I work,' said Tony. So he took me to his cookhouse. It was huge. Very spick and span inside; their cooking utensils were shining. Their barracks were spotless clean as well. Tony made me a pot of tea.

'I am cook here,' he said. 'I make the Commandant's breakfasts, lunch and tea.'

After I'd drunk my tea, we went into the large hall where a group of them were playing accordions, concertinas and Balalaikas. I thoroughly enjoyed the music. The majority of them had girlfriends; Karl's Bette was there and so was Daisy with Chris, as well as a few others I didn't know that well. When it got to about ten o'clock, I said I had to go for my bus and Tony walked me to the bus stop.

'See you at the dance on Saturday, Mary,' he said.

I nodded my head and came home.

As usual when I got in my Mother had supper ready for me.

'I've had a letter from our Barbara,' she told me. 'She wants us to come up to Falkirk for the weekend.'

'But I've made a date with Tony for the dance on Saturday,' I said.

'Oh honey, he might be married,' said my Mother.

'That never entered my head,' I said. 'If I thought that then he would be out. I would never go out with a married man.'

I saw Doreen at work the next day, and when she asked if I was going to the dance at the weekend, I told her:

'Doreen, I am going to Scotland Friday night with my Mother. Only for the weekend. I think my Pa is going too.'

'I'm going to the dance with my boyfriend,' she

told me, and then she asked if Tony was going to the dance.

'I was supposed to see him there,' I said. 'But as I've only gone out with him a few times it's nothing serious. He will probably find himself another girl.'

When I got home from work on Friday night my Mother and Father were ready to go. My Mum had left plenty to eat for my brother Norman and he was old enough to be left. I dashed upstairs, got a quick wash and changed out of my work clothes, and then we all got the bus back into Newcastle and boarded the train to Scotland.

I was not keen on going, I would have much rather have gone to a film or a dance. I thought it was a mean trick to play on Tony too. But it was only for two nights. I did think he would find himself another girl if I wasn't there and I did kind of like him but there was nothing I could do.

When we got to Scotland, my sister's husband, Jock, was waiting for us at Polmont station. It was only a short drive to their house from there and when we arrived at their house, my sister Barbara's little home was cosy and we settled down for a good bit chat. She asked what I was doing.

'Enjoying life, dancing, flirting.' I said.

'Who is it?' Barbara asked.

'A young man from Hamsterley,' I told her. 'They are from the Baltic States. He has been in the slave labour camps in Germany. They have had a rough time those lads. Lots have died.'

Of course my sister's husband, Jock, knew all about it as he had joined up at the start of the War and had been with the Eighth Army all through the Middle East, Italy, Sicily, Austria until they ended up in Germany right at the end of the War.

'How do you always get stuck with one of those lads?' my sister asked.

'They must think I have a kind face,' I said. 'I was supposed to meet him at the dance tomorrow night and here I am in Scotland, not at the dance.'

'You lucky thing,' said Barbara.

'You shouldn't have got married,' I told her. 'You could have stayed at home with my Mum too'

But Jock spoke up:

'We are happy,' he said.

'So am I,' I said to him, 'I am single and I like my life.'

'You're getting older,' said Barbara.

'I am eighteen and half,' I said. 'That is not old. I am enjoying life. Anyway, I was meeting him at the dance on Saturday but as I won't be there, he will probably find another girl. He is a good-looking lad so I do not think he will have any problem finding someone else. But that is enough about me. What about you?' I asked.

Barbara told me that she was a little more used to living in Scotland now that she had got to know her neighbours. She got on with them, which was good. So, she was happy.

We all had a good sleep that night; it was nearly nine o'clock when I woke up. After breakfast, my Father said he was going for a walk and I said I would go with him. We walked and somehow we must have cut through some private grounds because four great hound dogs came bounding over to us. They put their two front feet on our shoulders and we could not move.

'I think that they're going to eat us,' I said to my Dad.

'Don't move. Keep still,' he said.

'I can't move!' I told him.

Then the owner came across.

'This is private land,' she said.

My Father apologised: 'We're very sorry,' he told her, 'We're strangers here and we took the wrong path.'

We eventually made our way back to my sisters.

There was not much going on in Maddiston; it was a small village so no dances. The rest of the day and night passed and on the Sunday we all came home.

On the way back, I thought about Tony. I thought: 'Mary, that was one mean trick. However, when I get to work on Monday I shall get all the news.'

Norman was pleased to see us when we got back but I had an early night and never knew anything more until my Mother woke me for work on Monday morning. I'd had a really good sleep and felt very much awake and refreshed and ready for work. I had a good breakfast and then went for my bus where I met one of my friends who asked about my weekend.

'It was quiet,' I said.

'Your Tony was looking for you at the dance on Saturday,' she said. 'He came across and asked where you were. When he knew that you weren't at the dance he walked straight back out again and didn't come back.'

I never said anything.

For a few weeks I went to other dances. But Doreen was still with her boyfriend and one night she asked if I fancied going to Rowlands Gill dance.

I thought: 'Tony will have got another girlfriend by now,' so I said, 'Why not?'

I told my Mum that I was going back to the dance at Rowlands Gill.

Then I said to her: 'There's no way will I go out with a married man.'

She said, 'Our Mary, they have been away from home a long time.'

So, off I went to the dance and we were all enjoying ourselves when I got a tap on my shoulder. It was my Romeo.

'Hello Mary,' he said.

'Where have you been?' he asked.

'Tony, I do not go out with married men,' I told him.

He laughed.

'I not married. Who say this?'

I told him my Mother had said that he might be married and then he said:

'How can I be married? I was fourteen years when the Germans invaded my country Latvia, and brought us to Germany for the Concentration Camps. I have been in Germany for many years till the Americans freed us and asked us if we wanted to come and work in England.'

'Why did you not go home?' I asked.

'We not go home under Russian rule. When Russia moves out of our country, we all go back home and I go back to school.'

His English was improving; it was getting very good.

That Saturday night dance he never left me. He kept saying: 'I tell Mother I not married. Next time you do not come, I come to seek you.'

I agreed to meet him on Sunday night.

'I am working late tomorrow night,' Tony said. 'So we meet at my bus stop at 6 o'clock. You promise you come?'

'I will come,' I said.

He said, 'I make the Commandant's tea. Then four of us make sandwiches and cakes for five hundred men in the camp.'

Then he said to me:

'Mary, I think you not love me when you not come.'

I'd never thought of it like that. I thought: 'At fourteen years of age what would his Mam think, her boy dragged into those concentration camps. We didn't know the half of it. We were all cosy in our homes during the war and we enjoyed our teenage life.'

'And yet,' I thought, 'at fourteen years. God, really you are still a child in your heart and mind. You can never think like that. Tony must have had a broken heart. Not one but many.'

When I came home from the dance, my Mother was waiting as usual so that my brother and I could tell her all our news. So I sat down and told her that Tony was not married.

I said, 'He was in Germany at fourteen years of age and he wants to go back to school because he is very good at maths.'

'We're all friends then,' said my Mum.

'He's coming across to see you,' I said.

By now it was well past midnight and my Mother had had a full house with my Grandfather and my Uncle Joe for supper so she must have been getting tired. My brother Norman had come back home with a black eye through him playing rugby.

We all agreed it was a beaut, then I said to him:

'You're nuts, our Norman, for playing rugby. It's cruelty,' but Norman told me that it was good exercise.

He then told us that his mates and he had been invited to tea at one of his friend's houses earlier. He said that it had been him, Ginger and Wilfred. They were all good friends and rough rugby players. The lad who'd invited them was their friend, Don, and he lived in a great posh house. Apparently they'd gone into this big house and there was a beautiful lounge, and in the dining room was a dining table all set for tea.

Well I knew for a fact that our Norman was a great eater and so were Ginger and Wilf; fifteen stone each they were. So our Norman told us that they'd gone into the dining room, each of them telling the other how hungry they were, which I also knew to be true, after a rugby match our Norman could have eaten a horse. Don's Mother had told them all to sit down he said, and he was laughing:

'So we all sat down expecting some soup to start, then our lunch, and then a dessert afterwards like we get here, and I looked down at my plate and there was a slice a toast with three beans on it.'

He said: 'Ma, I was more hungry when we had finished eating than I was when we sat down.'

Well, my Mum and I were on the floor with laughing.

'So this is how they afford their posh houses,' I said.

When we'd finished laughing and Norman had eaten his supper, we all went to bed. As usual,

Sunday was a long lie-in for me and I got up at eight o'clock. My brother Norman slept longer but sometimes on a Sunday I would take a trip down the bank to see my Grandfather, or I'd walk along to my brother Alex's and fetch my little niece Sandra back to our house for a visit. She was a beautiful little girl, with long blonde ringlets, very old-fashioned looking and we all adored her. Poor soul. She had a tragic end through two incompetent Englishmen. I thank God many times that I never married a back-street lazy Englishman.

If Sandra were here, then when our Norman woke up, he'd take her across to the farm to show her the sheep and the horses. My Mum was always stewing over a gas stove to make the cakes and apple and date tarts for our teas later on, because on Sunday my brother Alex, his wife Jean and his other little daughter, Maureen, would come for their tea too. When my sister, Barbara, was down from Scotland with her husband, like she was this weekend, then it was actually a pretty full house.

Chapter 24
A Borrowed Bicycle

Now while all this was going on, I still got my letters from Oscar in Germany. Sometimes two letters a week, sometimes one and I wrote back to him. He told me that the jobs were very bad to get across there.

Oscar lived in Ostfan in Germany and I knew Achim lived in Baden Baden, although I'd never heard from Achim after Oscar. I did think he could have dropped a line to me but he obviously had a different type of personality to Mary's nature.

A letter from Oscar had arrived on the Friday, and at breakfast on Sunday morning my Mum had reminded me to reply to him, so I thought I'd better write a few lines back. He had got a job in his home town now, he wrote to me, and he ended his letter with, 'Mary, I will see you soon.'

So Oscar was thinking I would go to Germany to

be with him. Well that wasn't going to happen. I had no fancy at all for living in Germany and less for being married. But I wrote my letter to him saying that I was pleased he was back home with his family and had found a job, and that it was very sad about his brother having been captured in Russia, as he'd once told me that under Russian rule they would be sent to Siberia. But I never mentioned that I was still enjoying my life and I didn't tell him that I would never ever go to live in Germany much less think of marriage. Oh no. Not Mary. Not yet.

I finished my letter. We had a whopping lunch and I ate so much I couldn't move after my custard and jelly pudding. Time was marching on. I got myself ready to meet Tony and off I went.

At six o'clock, he was waiting for me at the bus stop. We walked up through Lord Gort's estate to the barracks, rows and rows of them.

'We go to my barracks,' said Tony, 'I introduce you to the Commandant.'

So I was introduced to the Commandant, his name was Morland, and then we went across to Tony's cookhouse. The two other cooks there said:

'Go Tony, take Mary to see the film, we have made everything for supper,' so we went off to the film hut and watched the film.

The hut was pretty full and they all had their girlfriends with them. I knew some of them. When the film was finished, Tony said:

'I take you home now, Mary.'

'You won't be able to catch a bus back,' I told him but he said:

'I will borrow bicycle. You sit on the crossbar and I take you home.'

Well it was a good job it was mostly downhill because pedalling that bicycle took some energy.

'How many times have you done this?' I asked him laughing; this was one way to get home.

We sailed through Rowlands Gill and were just coming through Lockhaugh when we saw a light. It was the policeman on his bicycle coming the other way. He stopped, and so of course, we had to stop as well. I was a bit nervous because, of course ,these lads weren't meant to be roaming around after curfew and Tony could have got into a lot of bother.

'Where do you think you're going?' the Policeman asked.

Well Tony's English was getting better but it wasn't that good, so I explained that I'd missed my bus and that Tony was taking me home. The Policeman sort of harrumphed at us.

'Taking you home, is he?' he said, and then he laughed. 'You two be careful. This isn't good transport.'

He was still laughing when we set off again.

'Good luck getting up Stampy Moss Bank,' he said as he rode off.

We got back to my Mother's a little after eleven o'clock.

'Come in for a cup of tea,' I told him, but Tony said:

'Mary, I go back to camp as it is getting late. I see you tomorrow.'

'Wednesday,' I said.

'I come to seek you at Mother's,' said Tony, and we said goodnight.

My sister, Barbara, was down from Scotland for the weekend again.

'You're late,' she said, when I got back in.

'I'm not,' I told her. 'You've a right nerve to say that. It's no different than if I had been to a dance, in fact I would have been later.'

Then because I was starting to get a bit angry at the way she was bossing me. I said:

'You used to come in later with your boyfriends. I've only gone out with three men: two Germans and one young man who has been in the Concentration Camps. Three in eighteen years. You went out with lots of boys.'

Jock, her husband, looked at me and my Mother gave me a look, as much as to say, 'Enough!' so I left it at that and ate my supper.

'See you in the morning.' I said when I went up to bed.

But my sister went back to Scotland on the Monday. It didn't matter. Like always, we had our little arguments, sisters do.

Chapter 25
The International Dance

Tony and I would go to dances, or sometimes, for a change, we'd go to see a film at Rowlands Gill on a Sunday night. There was one Sunday night when we were at the films and this young girl never looked at the screen; she spent the whole time watching Tony.

'Romeo, is she your girl?' she asked.

'Yes, this is my girlfriend,' said Tony. She never watched the film; she just kept asking him daft questions and calling him Romeo all night.

I said, 'Tony, I think she likes you.'

It was pretty cold when we came out from the film. Tony had a scarf on and the scarf was taken off and put around my neck.

'It will keep you warm,' he said.

'I'm not cold,' I said. 'But thank-you, I will look

after it.'

Tony offered to walk me home but I told him: 'No. Mary will catch the bus. It is too far for you to walk back to your camp. See you tomorrow.'

'Tomorrow I work in the cookhouse,' he said. 'But there is an International Dance on in Newcastle and we go there. I bought two tickets. The whole camp is going; there is a bus from our camp. You go Mary?'

I said, 'Yes, if you have two tickets, but tell me where in Newcastle this dance is.'

'It is on Friday night. I see before Friday night and I tell you,' Tony said, and we arranged to meet on Wednesday night.

By now we were at the bus stop and the bus was due. When it arrived, I got on and came home. Another weekend over and workday Monday next.

When Wednesday night came around, I made my way to Hamsterley and Tony was standing waiting for me at the bus stop. There was a film on in the hall that night and we made our way to his Camp. Lord Gort's estate was in a woodland area and we walked past the lodge where the gamekeeper lived, through the gates and up the drive until we came to Tony's small barrack hut.

Inside the hut there were four bunk beds, a stove, which was burning hot, and the radio playing. The place was immaculate; floor polished, all the beds made properly and not a speck of dust to be seen. He was pretty lucky only to have to share with three people: Sasha, Deddels and Karl, as the other huts were large and had about thirty beds in them. Mind you, the hut was usually full of people anyway, some with accordions or concertinas; it was never dull. When we went into the hut everyone in there said 'hello' and then asked if I was going to the dance on Friday night.

'I think so,' I said.

When we'd said 'hello' and had a bit of a chat to everyone in the hut, Tony said to me:

'Mary, we go to the cook-house,' and once we were in there he made us a cup of tea and opened up a tin of peaches and poured some cream over them.

Tony always made me something when I visited.

'None of us go hungry anymore,' he said. 'Not after Germany.'

'I don't believe in going hungry,' I told him, 'and it's very kind of you to invite me to have peaches and cream but I'm not hungry, so instead I shall drink your tea and you can tell me about the dance on Friday.'

Tony told me that the dance was in Newcastle and that he'd meet me beside my bus stop at Marlborough Crescent. I'd be able to get the camp bus back with them, he said.

When I got home I told my Mother that I'd be out late on Friday at the International Dance in Newcastle.

'I don't know what time I'll get home,' I said to her. 'Perhaps I should have refused to go.'

'Oh, go and enjoy it,' said my Mum. 'It'll be fun.'

Friday night came. I had a new dress, coat and shoes and just as he'd promised, Tony was waiting for me at Marlborough Crescent.

The dance was in town but the dance hall was up beside the RVI and it was one I'd never been to before. The hall was jam-packed with people, all of them babbling away in a different language. That didn't stop me having a lovely night and it wasn't until eleven-thirty that Tony walked me back to the bus that the camp had put on.

Actually, so many people had gone from Hamsterley that they'd put on several buses just to bring them back again and when the bus began to move, a great chorus of singing started up. They were all songs I'd never heard of, all of them in different languages but there were some good singers there and I enjoyed listening to them.

When we reached Winlaton Mill, Tony got off the bus with me.

'I see you safely home,' he said.

'It's a long walk back,' I told him.

But Tony told me that he was off work the next day and so could sleep until lunchtime. By the time we got to my house it was past one in the morning. This was very late for me, in fact the first time in my life I'd ever been out so late. But, as usual, my Mum was waiting up.

'I never heard so many foreigners in England!' I said to her while I had my supper. 'You'd never credit how many there were in that dance hall, all babbling away in their different languages. Everybody was glad to see each other, everyone shaking hands with everyone else.'

'So you enjoyed yourself then?' asked my Mum.

'Well, if I hadn't then I'd not have stayed so late, I'd have come home on the next bus,' I told her. 'Tony never left me either. He certainly looks after me. There were all different ones wanting to dance with me, but if someone wanted to dance with me then they had to ask Tony's permission and he wouldn't give it. He said to me: 'I say to them, find your own girl' and then they'd walk away.'

'They're certainly very different to us, Mum,' I said. 'There are these three brothers in the Camp but they didn't ask me to dance because they don't go out with girls. Tony told me that they come home on a Friday night with their weekly wages and the eldest brother takes it from them and gives them their pocket money for the week. They are definitely different to English men.'

After telling my Mother all the news, off we went to bed and I slept like a log until the sun came peeking through the window. When I got up, there was a letter waiting for me from my friend Oscar in Germany. I thought he would have forgotten me and found another young lady in his own country. But no, he was still writing to me, still wanting me to go across to Germany and marry him.

'I think they take their girls too serious,' I said to my Mum after I'd finished reading the letter.

'Well honey,' said my Mother, 'not everyone is like Mary Hymers; here today and gone tomorrow.'

Saturday rolled around again.

'Where to tonight?' asked my Mum while I was having breakfast.

'I'm off to see a film,' I told her. 'I will be home soon tonight.'

That afternoon Doreen came across.

'Where you off to tonight?' she asked. 'I'm going out with my boyfriend,' because she was still seeing that English bloke she'd met at Rowlands Gill dance.

'I'm going to see a picture,' I said to her.

'Oh, go to the dance,' she said.

'Not after last night's dance,' I said to her. 'Tonight I'm having an early night.'

'Oh well, I have a date so I will see you at work on Monday,' said Doreen.

I walked her to the door.

'See you on Monday,' I said as I waved her off.

Soon after Doreen left, my other two friends, Mary and Joyce, arrived.

'I haven't seen you for ages,' I told them. 'Do you still hear from your friend across the sea?'

'No,' they said. 'We both have boyfriends now,

English ones. What about you Mary?'

'I still hear from Oscar,' I said to them. 'In fact, he wants me to go across to Germany to live.'

They were both aghast at the news.

'Of course, I'm not going,' I told them. 'I met this lad, Tony, at Rowlands Gill dance and I've gone out with him a few times. He was one of the young men they brought over from the Concentration Camps in Germany.'

'What's he like?' they asked, and we settled down to a good chat.

'He's rather nice and I like him,' I said to them. 'It's peculiar isn't it? When everyone had gone away I would say to myself; I'm going to be stuck with an English chap. Maybe it's my make-up, inside of me. But instead, I met Tony. He comes from Latvia, Riga. I really like him. But then every boyfriend I've gone out with I've really liked or else I'd not have gone out with them.'

We all began to smile.

I said, 'We had some good fun didn't we?'

'Yes. We had a few good laughs,' they said.

Before they left, Joyce and Mary made me promise to come to see them. I said I would and then off they went and it was time to go and meet Tony. I told my Mum I'd be back soon that night and asked her to come and meet me at about ten-thirty in Winlaton Mill.

'Your Dad and I will walk down to seek you,' she

promised.

Off I went to Rowlands Gill and Tony was waiting for me.

'Where are we going? To the dance, Mary?' he asked.

'Not tonight,' I said. 'I am having an early night. We go see a film.'

It was a good film, and by the time it finished it was pretty dark outside.

'It is too early to go home,' Tony said.

'My Mother is meeting me at Winlaton Mill about ten-thirty. By the time I get home it will be eleven o'clock, so not so early,' I told him.

'I will take you home,' he said.

'You did plenty of walking last night from Winlaton to Hamsterley.' I said. 'It's a fair hike.'

Tony said, 'I do not mind. I am not a prisoner any more. I am free and I can walk into my camp at any time.'

'That's good,' I told him. 'But my limit is eleven o'clock or a little bit later through the week, and at the weekend my Mother knows my dances finish later on a Friday, Saturday and Sunday. If I'm going to be very late then I have to tell her first.'

'I walk you to Lockhaugh then.'

His English was much better; he was quick at learning, and so we walked to Lockhaugh for my bus.

'Will you marry me?' he asked.

I had to turn my face away as I was about to giggle.

'I hardly know you,' I said.

'You not love me then,' he said.

At that, I said then, as I had always thought.

'I am too young to die. Married? God no. Marriage never enters my head.'

'What you mean too young to die?' Tony asked.

'Just that,' I said. 'Marriage is out.'

'Then you do not love me,' he said.

'Right,' I told him. 'We talk about something' and then I said: 'Romeo, at the minute I am enjoying life. No marriage, only good friends.'

'I come to meet you at home,' Tony said. 'Tomorrow night.'

'Anytime,' I said.

'I tell meine Mother, I not married,' he told me.

I laughed. 'I believe you.'

'I tell her,' he said. 'I come to seek you at home tomorrow.'

By now my bus had arrived at the bus stop and I boarded it and got off at the Mill, where my Mum and Dad were waiting for me. It was a beautiful night, the moon and stars were out and I linked my Mum and Dad all the way up the spooky road through the fields to Winlaton.

Chapter 26
Tony's Story

Sunday night came and there was a knock on the front door and when I opened it, Tony was standing there.

'Come in, Tony,' said my Mum.

My Dad was sitting in his armchair beside the fire.

'Good evening, meine Mother. Good evening, mein Father,' Tony said.

'Sit down, Tony,' said my Mum. 'We're just going to have a cup of tea.'

Tony sat down with us

'Mother, I not married,' he said, and my Mum just looked at me.

'I fourteen years of age when Germans invaded my country, and I in prison camps until the Americans freed us. I come from Riga in Latvia. It is a country that is ruled by Russia: not a free country. Not yet. When Russia moves out, we go home. Meine Mother and Father are still alive and I have three brothers: Edward, Sigmund and Stanislav. I had a young sister too but she died when she was seven from the typhoid. My oldest brother Edward, he is dead too. He died when the Germans invaded my country. He twenty. When the Germans came, I had just finished school for the day and I was taking my dog Susie for a walk. The German soldiers came up to me and said 'You come with us'. They shoot my little Susie. I shouted to a neighbour, 'Tell my Mama they are taking me away' and they took me to the railway station. There were thousands of us. The last time I saw my Mama she was beside the station gates and she was shouting to me. I could not hear what she says. The last thing my Mama shout at me I cannot hear. She was crying and so was I. I was not allowed to go to her. The gates were shut. There were big cattle trucks and they made us climb into them. We could not move; we were so many in each truck. We had nothing to eat. For days we eat nothing.'

Tony told us that when they reached Munich they were told to get out of the trucks and taken to a place where they were fumigated for lice. Then they were fed a little. After that, they were placed in camps. Polish, Lithuanians, Yugoslavians; all nationalities were there. They were kept there for a few months and then they were taken to different camps and made to work as slave labour on the railways.

'My heart was broken,' he said. 'I do not see meine Mother and Father. We had to sleep with our clothes on, so they were not stolen. We were cold, so cold in winter. There was no food. We were always hungry and the Germans were there all the time. Standing over us. Watching us. Counting us. In the prison camps there were thousands. Ten's of thousands. All speaking their own language. But, as the years go, I speak a few languages: Russian, Polish, Hungarian, Lithuanian. I speak good German and now I am learning English.'

Of course, my Father was all ears at what Tony was saying.

'Do you write home, Tony?' my Dad asked.

'No. I not write the time Russian rule my country,' Tony said.

'We don't know the half of it,' said my Mother.

'So you see Mother, Father,' said Tony. 'I am not married and so I look after Mary.'

'That's very kind of you, Tony,' I thought. 'But Mary can look after Mary.'

But all I said was: 'Tony, we'll go to see a film.'

'Come back for your supper, Tony,' said my Mum.

When we came out from the film we went back to my Mum's and Tony had his supper but it was a dash, as I didn't want him to miss his last bus and have to walk back to Hamsterley from Winlaton.

I walked to the bus stop with him.

'Tomorrow night, Mary,' said Tony.

'Wednesday,' I said to him.

'Wednesday is a long time, I come to seek you tomorrow night at Mother's,' he said.

I thought: 'I'm going out with the girls tomorrow night,' but I told him:

'It's a rush for me from when I arrive home from work to go out again. I will see you on Wednesday, Tony.'

'I work on Wednesday until eight o'clock,' said Tony. 'I come to meet you at my bus-stop after I finish.'

I said: 'If you are working, I'll meet you at Burnopfield dance on Saturday night instead.'

'No,' said Tony. 'I like to see you,' and I thought, 'They must really get fed up with camp life"

Monday morning and it was back to work as usual. There was always hustle and bustle and work for everyone, no one lazed around or shirked. Why would you want to if you were capable of a good day's work? You could take your pick of jobs: engineering, ship-workers, foundry work or factory work like my job at Sinclair's. It was all young girls like me who worked there and for good wages, too. During the war, we got a productivity bonus every three-month from Mr Sinclair which paid for a new rig-out for me. The only fault I could pick with working at Sinclair's was that if you got married then they finished you working there.

On the Monday, my friends were all going on about the dance at Blaydon Church Hall.

'Are you coming, Mary?' they asked.

'Sure,' I said.

Monday night coming out of our factory was one mad rush for the bus home; we came pouring out of the doors like flies, and the queues when we all reached the bus stop were massive. But buses came pouring in at Marlborough Crescent and the crowds soon disappeared.

When we got home it was tea, quick wash to get the dust off, change clothes and then on with our lipstick, powder, earrings and bracelets and that was us out of our working clothes and all toffed up to go to our dance. There was a dramatic change in our appearance, from drudges into first class models. Mind you, the clothes were nicer then, the material better. You had yards of material in your dresses. Chiffon blouses, pleated skirts, silk stockings with black seams up the back and sometimes butterflies on the ankles too, just hovering above our suede shoes. We never heard of trousers. I'd never worn a pair and neither had the other girls.

We had a great time at the dance, and after it had finished we all came out and walked back home. As we got along to Blaydon we passed the church clock, it was after eleven o'clock. My brother Norman and his two friends, Ginger and Wilf, were sitting on the church wall as they usually did. Ginger and Wilf were on night shift at the pit and so they went off to get ready for their work and Norman walked back home with me and my friends.

As we walked off, Ginger and Wilf shouted after us:

'See you in the morning, Norm.'

'Will do,' said Norm, but when they'd gone, he said:

'Tomorrow morning when I am going to work Ginger and Wilf are coming off night-shift and they shout at me, 'See you the night Norm.' They make good money in the pit and here's me serving my time to be an engineer and my pocket money from my job doesn't match their large pocket money from their pit-work.'

It was true what he said. To be an engineer meant serving your time from when you left school at fourteen until you were twenty-one and as an apprentice you didn't get a big pay packet.

When we got back into the house, I had my supper and a cup of tea and then I said: 'I'm off to bed,' because I was up at six the next morning for work.

When you think about it, we had a good long shift, what with working, dancing, you could guarantee we didn't get much sleeping. But I suppose we were healthy and we ate very well. We always, but always, had good food. As the butcher Norman Tweddle used to say to my Mother, 'Sina, you're the best provider in Winlaton.' I'd say she was the best cook in Winlaton too. 'You can't build a good castle on a bad foundation' my Mum would say. It started with breakfast in the morning. My Mother would shout up the stairs: 'Mary, Norman, time to rise' and with much sleep in our eyes we would get out of bed, get washed, dressed and then have our breakfast. My Mum would be at the table already with the teapot ready to pour, sugar and milk on the table too, as we all took sugar in our tea. Breakfast was bacon and eggs and our lunches were already packed ready for us when we went out of the door. If we fancied going to the canteen at work then my Mother would give us the money but I liked my packed lunches.

So as I said, it was a short sleep and then it was Tuesday and back to work for another day.

When I saw my friends at lunchtime and they asked me, 'Mary, where are you going tonight?' I told them: 'Home for a very early night. I feel shattered.'

They all agreed with me too; it was a night for washing our hair and relaxing and that's what I did when I got back home from work: hair-wash, tea and an hour's relaxing and then bed at nine o'clock on the dot where I slept like a log until my Mother wakened me for work the next morning.

Back at work and every one of my friends asked the same question.

'Where to tonight?'

Doreen said: 'I have a young man to meet.'

I told them that I was meeting Tony. When work was done it was the same mad rush for the bus home, tea and then out again.

I met Tony at about seven-thirty that night. He was waiting for me at the bus stop as he'd promised and we walked to his cookhouse.

'I nearly finished my work,' he told me, so I sat and

had a cup of tea while he finished up.

While we were in there Karl came into the cookhouse with his girlfriend, Bette. Karl and Tony were great pals and shared the same barracks and they were chattering away to each other in their own language; Tony was speaking to Karl, while Bette and I sat there and drank our tea.

Bette was very dressy in her appearance but nice looking with it and although I didn't know her very well, I'd met Karl a few times and he was a very happy-go-lucky sort of chap, good fun and a great dancer. They stayed for a while and then got up to go.

'I'll see you later, Mary,' said Bette as they left.

'Is something wrong Tony?' I asked when they'd gone, because it had seemed that after a while Tony had been doing all of the talking while Karl just laughed at what he was saying.

Tony said: 'I tell him to get a single girl.'

'Is Bette not single?' I asked, and Tony said no, then he told me that she had left her husband for Karl.

'I tell Karl he makes much trouble. I said it is not my business but I have known him a long time and I keep him right. We all help each other.'

'Well it's good when you all help each other,' I told him.

'We have to,' said Tony. 'We all look after each other. I tell Karl, "Bette's husband will come after you," but Karl laughs it off. He said he loves her.'

By now, Tony had finished his work.

'Come Mary, we see some of the film,' he said, so we went into the big hall and watched some of the film.

By now it was getting on for nine o'clock and when the film was over Tony said:

'Mary I bought a new radio, we can go into my barracks and I can tune into different programmes.'

I knew that Tony liked music, the majority of his pals played accordions and concertinas and he told me that two of his brothers played the accordion although his youngest brother Stanislav did not, so we walked across to his barracks which as usual were warm and cosy and spotless clean.

Karl was in there with Bette and it was getting late, so I said to Tony: 'By the time I walk down to the bus stop it will be ten o'clock and I must catch my bus. My Mum will be waiting for me at the bus stop.'

'I take you home, Mary,' offered Tony, but I refused, telling him:

'No, I'll catch my buses.'

We walked down to the bus stop together.

'I see you tomorrow?' Tony asked.

'Not tomorrow. Saturday night,' I told him.

'No, I come see you tomorrow,' he said.

'Alright, you can come to my house,' I told him.

I was home before eleven o'clock and as I ate my supper, I said to my Mum:

'You're getting company tomorrow.'

'Honey,' said my Mother. 'These young men in the camps are lucky to be here. Tony can come any time he likes.'

So the next night, Tony came to visit me at home and we had supper together.

The next Saturday we went up to Burnopfield for the dance. The nights were getting darker but inside, the dance hall was all lit-up and with the dance band and the silvery lights; it was magical. Everybody knew everyone else and we were all friendly with each other. Tony arrived with Karl and few more from Hamsterley Camp and Bette was already there, waiting for Karl.

'Karl is going to tell Bette he is not seeing her anymore,' Tony told me.

I said to him: 'I don't know Bette really but she should stay with her husband. Karl can look for a single girl anytime. But, whatever happens, it will all work out like everything always does.'

But being truthful about it, from the way that Karl ran around Bette, you could tell that he liked her, and for all she was married you could tell that Bette really liked Karl as well. I think that she must have been married very young because she wasn't that much older than I was, she would only be in her early twenties.

I heard later that Bette's husband did go to see

Karl to find out what was going on but even that didn't stop the two of them meeting. Karl was a very carefree sort of person and wouldn't have listened to either Tony or Bette's husband, and in fact, Bette did leave her husband for Karl; one night she'd just packed her bags and left and went up to the camp to stay with Karl but Tony said to him: 'She can't stay here.'

You would have thought her own brains would have told her that she couldn't go to stay in a camp with all those hundreds of men, and so of course she had to go back to her husband.

After Karl and Bette stopped seeing each other I never saw Karl with another woman, not until a few years later when he moved to Doncaster to work in the mines and married a girl he met down there. But that didn't last long and so Karl and Bette must really have loved each other.

Chapter 27
We Get Married

By now I had been courting Tony for twelve months and he was always asking me: 'Mary, we get married?'

'You have no job, Tony,' I'd tell him, but he never gave up asking.

'I look for one,' he would say. 'All our boys are looking for jobs. When I get a job, we get married.'

Eventually I gave in and we did get married. I was twenty years of age and I wore a green dress with a black three-quarter-length coat in the New Look style. We had a simple service at the Anfield Plain registry office and my brother Norman and Tony's great friend, Karl, stood as our witnesses.

We moved into a one-bedroomed terraced house on Rectory Lane near to St Pauls Church and Tony's first job in England was at Consett brickworks.

I had a bicycle that my father had bought for me

when I'd been seeing Oscar and as I'd hardly ever used it, it was practically brand-new. So Tony used it for getting up to his job in Consett. He would leave our home at four o'clock in the morning so that he could arrive at the Brickworks ready to start his shift at six. It was an awfully long hike from Winlaton, about fourteen miles each way and all uphill on the way there. To get to the bottom of Medomsley Bank from Winlaton was about eight miles and then the long pull up the bank and through Medomsley to Consett.

'You won't feel like it,' I told him.

'It's alright coming back,' Tony told me. 'But getting up Medomsley Bank in winter is hard work.'

I said, 'Tony, we have to find you another job.'

Now Tony was clever and spoke five languages and so he was offered a place in London, in the Russian Embassy as an interpreter. However I had no fancy to go and live in London and so we didn't go, even though I knew that it would have been a good job and Tony would have made pots of money.

Instead, he kept on with the job at Consett Brickworks, the long hill, and the early mornings. God love him, he was up before it was light and back home after it was dark and every morning before he left, he laid the fire in the kitchen so that all I had to do was set a match to it and it was lit, and my little house was warm and cosy.

The months moved by and one year later, we had our little boy Tony. It was pretty hard when we were first married but my Tony was good with his money and gave me all his pay packet every week. I got his pay packet every week until the day he retired.

By now, the camp at Hamsterley was broken up and all Tony's pals from the camp moved down to Doncaster to work in the coal mines.

One night, Tony said to me:

'Mary, I go to Doncaster to work in the mines. Karl has got me a job there and I have to go for this job. I have to work for you and the boys tell me that I will get a house down there once I start to work.'

'Well,' I said, 'You do that and I will look around for a little job. My Mother will look after young Tony,' because of course as soon as I'd got married I had been laid off my job at John Sinclair's.

Tony went to Doncaster and started to work in the mines and he wrote to me every day telling me how he was getting on. After a month, he wrote to tell me that he had found us a house. But I still had no fancy in going to Doncaster and I didn't want him to work in the mines so I wrote back to him saying: 'Come home Tony,' and Tony handed his notice in at the coal mine and came back home.

When Tony came home, he said to me: 'Mary, I not like coal mines.'

'I don't want you to work in the coal mines,' I told him. 'You are better than that.'

My brother Norman, who was now twenty-one, was just finishing serving his time as an apprentice engineer while my oldest brother, Alex, had finished doing his studies at night school and was now District Manager of different coal mines and so they were both doing very well with good jobs.

But what to do about Tony? I really didn't want him to work in the mines but we did need to have money coming in and so my Father said: 'I will get him a job with me at Smith Patterson's.'

My Dad was as good as his word and got him a job at Smith Patterson's in Blaydon. Tony liked his job at the factory and being able to save up a little bit of money meant that he could buy a motorbike and side-car and so he and my Father would go to work together every day.

My Dad was past retirement age but he still worked a twelve-hour shift as ambulance man and storekeeper at Smith Patterson's, so when Tony finished work at five o'clock, my Dad would be at work until seven. To save my Father from having to wait to catch a bus back home, Tony would drive back down to Blaydon to seek him when his shift was finished.

'Mien Father works long hours, so he is tired,' Tony would say.

They got on well, my Dad and Tony. They would go for a drink together and were the best of pals. My Dad always said: 'It does not matter who I am with, I am his Father.'

Tony kept in with my Mother too. He'd do anything for them, take them wherever they wanted to go, mend whatever needed to be fixed. If we had a tiff he would say: 'Father, it is Mary's fault, she started it,' but my Father was never one to judge anyone. He'd always say: 'Hinny, there are two ends to every stick.'

Of course my Mum had said: 'I'll look after young Tony if you want to find a job,' when I mentioned that I was thinking of going back to work which was a great help.

After Tony had come back from Doncaster, I got a job working for my mother's cousin Mrs Jenny Leck. Her maiden name was Dance and my old Granny was a Dance before she married my Grandfather, Alexander Gilfillan. My old Granny was Jenny's Aunt Emma.

Jenny had come to my mum's house and she was just saying: 'Sina, do you know of anyone who would work in my husband's garage serving petrol to cars and doing their oil for them,' when I walked in.

My Mother said: 'Our Mary is looking for a job,' and Jenny asked if I'd like to work for them at her husbands garage.

'I could give it a try,' I said to her.

They lived at the crossroads in Crawcrook and it took me two buses to get there. One to Ryton and then another one to Crawcrook. The job was great and I got the hang of serving petrol and oil, and Jenny and her husband were very kind to me. But the two buses got to me. I left the house at seven in the morning and I never got back home until six-thirty at night, and so I only stuck it one month. I could not handle the two buses.

Standing in the rain one night, I thought: 'This is it,' and so the very next day I said to Jenny:

'I am sorry Jenny, but my Mum is doing my husband's dinners for him and she's looking after young Tony. She has my Uncle Joseph to look after too since my Grandfather died. It's too much for her and I'm not going to let her keep on doing it all.'

So, that was the end of me working at the Petrol Station.

My first proper job after I was married was with Thornton Bullerwell. I worked a lot of years for Thornton and there were some hard-working land girls worked with me: Kathleen, Tilly, and Phyllis. God they could graft. I stooked corn and threshed turnips, and I mean fields of turnips. I did it when the frost was biting into your fingertips and the leaves were hard with ice and your back was bent down to the ground for miles. I picked potatoes, mucked cows, fed them. Believe you me, I never thought I could do it. I wasn't used to such graft and I thought I would never be able to tackle it.

But as the years rolled on I got used to it, in fact I quite enjoyed being in the fresh air all day and there were many farmers who came to seek us to work for them if we weren't busy at Thornton's farm. Even Thornton Bullerwell's brother, Tommy, would say to me: 'Mary, leave our Thornton and come and work with me.'

After a few years with Thornton, he asked me if I would like to deliver milk so I did that. It was good money. I'd get up at four in the morning to begin work at five and I'd travel round with the milk float. There was only one fault with the job. I would do the girls' day off, three days in the week. But, as they all had different delivery rounds, I had to have a jolly good memory, to be able to learn the different doors and deliver the right order: a gill of milk here, a pint of milk there. However, after a few weeks I sharp got the hang of it.

We were able to get a council house on Tyne Bank, just down from where my Mother and Father lived. I loved that house. Even though it was a council house, it was quite large, with a lovely garden front and back, French windows in the dining room and a wood-burning stove. Our neighbours were nice too. We lived next door to Mrs Simpson. She had six in her family, five sons and a daughter Brenda. The youngest of her boys, Lindsey, was great friends with my son Tony.

My mother was still looking after my son Tony while I was at work. In fact, she wouldn't part with him, but she was like this with everyone's child; she was the same with our Alex's daughter Sandra. She'd take them all on holiday with her to see my sister, Barbara, up in Scotland. Barbara only had one son too, Alex, who was a year older than young Tony. Alex and Tony were great pals all their teenage life.

I was still working on the milk float for Thornton

Bullerwell, the farmer. It wasn't a bad job and at least I didn't have to travel into Newcastle ever day. Some of the other married girls I knew had to leave home for their jobs at eight o'clock in the morning and didn't get back home until six o'clock at night. I didn't want that. I wanted to be home to cook all of the meals so that they were ready to go on the table when Tony came home from work and young Tony came back from school. That was how my Mum had done things; we had never had to wait for our dinners, they were always ready for us to sit down to. So I made sure that all of my jobs were on the doorstep, so that I could be home in time to do that.

They had started to build Leech's houses on the fields across from where my Mother lived, the fields where I had first seen Achim and where Mrs Snarr and her boys had farmed. As they were being built, I would look at them and think: 'I wonder if they want a cleaner?'

After a while I went and asked the foreman if there were any cleaning jobs going. He said that they needed a cleaner to go in after the builders had finished. It was good money. Over twice what I was getting from working on the milk. Three pounds a bungalow and four pounds for a house. The more houses I could clean, the more money I would get.

I left working for Thornton and started cleaning the houses. When the workmen had finished with the building work, I would go into the new house with pails of hot water. They were filthy dirty. Paint on the windows, cement stuck to the wooden floors.

The toilets and the baths still had their covering of thick brown paper, which had to be scrubbed off with a hard scrubbing brush. Where the painters had spattered paint on the big picture windows I had to take a wallpaper scraper and scrape the paint off with that. It was hard work.

'Christ,' I thought, 'I should have stayed on the milk.'

THE END

www.ingramcontent.com/pod-product-compliance
Lightning Source LLC
Chambersburg PA
CBHW050534300426
44113CB00012B/2093